D0629758

Copyright © 2019 by Dylan Howard and Andy Tillett

All rights reserved. No part of this book may be reproduced in any manner without the express written consent of the publisher, except in the case of brief excerpts in critical reviews or articles. All inquiries should be addressed to Skyhorse Publishing, 307 West 36th Street, 11th Floor, New York, NY 10018.

Skyhorse Publishing books may be purchased in bulk at special discounts for sales promotion, corporate gifts, fund-raising, or educational purposes. Special editions can also be created to specifications. For details, contact the Special Sales Department, Skyhorse Publishing, 307 West 36th Street, 11th Floor, New York, NY 10018 or info@skyhorsepublishing.com.

Skyhorse® and Skyhorse Publishing® are registered trademarks of Skyhorse Publishing, Inc.®, a Delaware corporation.

Visit our website at www.skyhorsepublishing.com.

10 9 8 7 6 5 4 3 2 1

Library of Congress Cataloging-in-Publication Data is available on file.

Jacket design by 5mediadesign
Cover photo credit: The Mega Agency

Print ISBN: 978-1-5107-5508-6

Printed in the United States of America

THE LAST CHARLES MANSON TAPES

EVIL LIVES BEYOND THE GRAVE

DYLAN HOWARD
ANDY TILLETT

Skyhorse Publishing

TABLE OF CONTENTS

Introduction *iv*

Chapter One 1

Chapter Two 17

Chapter Three 31

Chapter Four 51

Chapter Five 65

Chapter Six 81

Chapter Seven 103

Chapter Eight 135

Chapter Nine 149

Chapter Ten 169

Appendix: Manson: The Final Interview, January 2017 *183*

INTRODUCTION

Charles Manson's restless, manic, murderous eyes pierce through you—off the magazine page, out of court footage, through the years, through history.

Those eyes pierce all the way from 1969, when Manson ordered his brain-washed and drug-addled band of hippie kids to savagely murder seven people in a two-night orgy of violence, which shook America to its foundations, led Hollywood to start locking their doors, and in one stroke killed the peace and free love hippie movement.

The killings left seven cadavers stabbed so many times, gallons of their blood oozed across the floors of their luxury homes.

Chilling messages were daubed at the crime scenes—PIG, HEALTER SKELTER, and POLITICAL PIGGY—puzzling "clues" which would baffle cops and only add to the panic and delirium created by the scenes where they were scrawled. They were meant to herald a war which would signal the beginning of the end times.

The Manson Family slaughtered the affluent and famous as barbarically and indifferently as the everyday people they also chose as victims.

The murderers lived in a series of sordid communes as a ragged band of 30—taking LSD, hosting orgies and complying with whatever Charlie said. And Charlie didn't mince his words. Although he would later downplay his involvement in the murders, one of his disciples, Dianne Lake, readily described how he had taught female followers to stab victims in the chest and to "rip up" so their knives would hit the most of the body's vital organs and cause maximum pain and damage.

The Manson murders provided some of the goriest images in an era studded with shocking crimes, from the assassinations of John F. Kennedy, Martin Luther

King, and Robert Kennedy to the senseless and brutal stabbing death of Kitty Genovese on a New York street in 1964, as pedestrians passively looked on.

The Manson Family killings grabbed headlines away from events of magnitude in the newspapers and evening news: race riots, the Vietnam war, the moon landing.

The Manson-led horrors which would captivate America came to public attention on August 9, 1969. The day before, beautiful actress Sharon Tate, 26, the wife of rising film director Roman Polanski, had been two short weeks from giving birth. She left her hilltop home, 10050 Cielo Drive in Los Angeles, for a dinner with friends at El Coyote Mexican restaurant in Hollywood, which still operates to this day.

The group returned to the Tate-Polanski home at around 10:30 and then all hell broke loose as a black-clad team of merciless and unstoppable demon hippies descended to kill them all—seemingly for no reason.

The carnage was absolute. It was slow, sadistic, painful, and utterly without mercy. It was the climax of years of brooding and degeneracy, the real-world manifestation of the mad visions of a self-proclaimed messiah.

Serial murders like those carried out by the Manson Family were practically unheard of at the time. As more of his story became known, Manson earned himself a place alongside the most infamous figures in *world* history, such as Jack the Ripper and Adolf Hitler.

Charles Manson was a monster. And yet, merged with the flood of change—from flower children to the Vietnam War, from the Woodstock music festival to the militant Black Panthers—he became a symbol of a turbulent era. He may well have given the '60s counterculture its ultimate symbol.

* * *

Charles Manson strove to become a subversive, mind-controlling renegade without anything approaching a moral compass—the very definition of a villain, a title he accepted and relished.

His most notorious photographs are instantly recognizable—a captivatingly wild-eyed figure, a shaggy rebel not unlike Che Guevara, cuffed and led by police.

They appear on a variety of merchandise aimed at those who feel being disassociated from society is something to be celebrated.

There were, and still are, "followers" who consider Manson a hero—perhaps intrigued by the more gruesome aspects of the Family's murders, or the fact they happened in the bright, shiny picture-perfect heart of America's glamorous entertainment industry—Hollywood. Or maybe they are just people angry and jealous of the successful, rich and attractive, who feel murder is a valid way of getting their own back.

Certainly the four people butchered by the Family in the early hours of August 9, 1969, were part of the "in" crowd.

Sharon Tate was an actress whose accolades for her talent and her great beauty had steadily been getting louder.

Jay Sebring's empire of men's grooming services was flourishing.

Abigail Folger, the heiress to a fortune, was a much-revered socialite.

And Wojciech Frykowski (pronounced Voytek)—was a young friend of Tate's husband, Roman Polanski, who was trying to scratch out his place in Hollywood.

In contrast, the couple killed by the Family the next night, Leno and Rosemary LaBianca, were older and publicly anonymous. But they had made a fortune through hard work and had been looking forward to their retirement.

Clues and messages at the Tate/LaBianca crime scenes hinted at a larger, sinister motivation, although it's hard to pinpoint what, as the group's acid-soaked beliefs and Manson's prison-learned pseudo-philosophical ramblings never added up to much.

But Manson was a charismatic leader and studied con-man who knew how to say what people desperately wanted to hear. Therein, perhaps, lies Manson's greatest dark attraction. He was a small, slight man—arrest records show him at five foot seven, taller than the five foot two some sources ascribe to him. For Manson, bullying people through brute force was less effective than warping their minds.

Manson also knew whom to choose. There is a common thread among the people he controlled. Many came from shattered home lives, or had already been heavily using drugs, or otherwise had their senses of self-worth destroyed. He sought followers who were already damaged, then broke them even further.

Manson may, on some level, have convinced himself he was a hero. As he told counterculture satirist and journalist Paul Krassner, he brought people who had already been discarded by society into a family-like structure. What he encouraged them to do afterward—to completely submit to his dominance—is where the horror lies. He even viewed the word "why" as a direct challenge to his authority and bullied the word out of his followers' mouths.

Given the sheer number of people in the Family—between a dozen and thirty hardcore members, and up to one hundred on the fringes—there are numerous interpretations of events, a whole host of acid-casualty unreliable narrators.

Through the accounts of those who were there, their friends, police reports, court testimony and interviews, *this* is the definitive account of the madness of Charles Manson.

It shows how he formed his merry band of hippie killers, forced himself into the media spotlight and went completely insane under it, dying in 2017 after a lifetime of defiance and rage against authority, but leaving an indelible mark on American culture.

As one of his jail confidants would later reveal: "He knew his influence and how big he was. Sometimes he'd say 'Ted Bundy was a coward'—and then tell you he, Manson, was the greatest serial killer of all time.

"I asked him directly what he thought he should be diagnosed with and he'd say: 'I'm everything. I'm schizophrenic, I'm bipolar . . . I'm a psychopath.'"

CHAPTER ONE

Your mother teaches you why, why, why. You go around asking your mother why and she keeps telling you, "Because, because," and she laces your little brain with because and: "Because." "Why?" "Because." "Why?" And you don't know any different. If you had two mothers, one to tell you one thing and one to tell you another, then your mind might be left where mine was.

—CHARLES MANSON, COURT STATEMENT, NOVEMBER 19, 1970

Charles Milles Manson was born on November 12, 1934, in Cincinnati, Ohio into an already broken home and a flawed life.

Manson's mother, Kathleen Maddox, was a party girl. At fifteen in early 1934, she was chafing against the strict evangelical upbringing pushed by her mother, Nancy. Modest dress, no makeup, social activities limited to church-related functions and above all, no dancing.

But Kathleen frequently escaped from the Family home in northern Kentucky into Ohio, to the dance halls and bars friendly to teenage girls, just far enough away that stories of her behavior would not follow her home.

Kathleen—whose father, Charlie Milles Maddox, had died suddenly in 1931—flirted, played and had sex.

Was Kathleen a prostitute, as her son Charlie Manson would later claim? There are no records of her being picked up for solicitation, but she would frequently be found in the bars and flop houses frequented by sex workers and other unsavory characters. Like so many of Manson's self-reported biographical details, the story was likely a spin designed to gain sympathy.

Kathleen was from an unlucky family. Her older brother Luther dabbled in larceny and her older sister Glenna had a curious choice in men (her first husband was hot tempered, her second a drinker). A second sister, Aileene, had died two years after her father.

Then Kathleen became pregnant at age 15. The father was likely Colonel Walker Henderson Scott, a charmer who was happy to let people think his given name indicated military service. He was also happy to have the attention of a girl eight years younger than himself. But he was not happy about being a father, and upon being told Kathleen was carrying his child he promptly vanished—likely back to his wife, Dorothy.

By the time of Charles Maddox's birth, however, Kathleen had found another suitor: William Manson, a Cincinnati resident she had met during one of her forays into Ohio, whom she quickly wed, lying about her age to say she was 21, despite still being 15—and six months pregnant.

Upon the arrival of Charles Milles Manson, a temporary birth certificate given to Kathleen at the hospital listed no first name. After she decided to call him Charles, the official birth certificate kept at the Ohio Department of Vital Statistics recorded his full name, with William Manson listed as his father.

Although married, Kathleen was hardly settled. She continued to go out dancing, drinking, and enjoying herself, leaving young Charlie with neighbors or various family relatives, sometimes not returning for him for several days. Less than six months after their marriage, William Manson left Kathleen and later filed for divorce in 1936, stating the marriage had been childless, effectively removing himself from any responsibility for Charlie's upbringing.

According to some sources, so did Kathleen. When he grew up, Charlie Manson would tell a story which he attributed to family lore. He claimed Kathleen had brought him as an infant into a bar. A waitress kiddingly said she would love a child of her own, to which Kathleen allegedly responded, "a pitcher of beer and he's yours." Kathleen finished the beer and split, leaving Manson's uncle to track down the waitress and bring him home.

Next, Kathleen teamed with brother Luther in petty crime. On the evening of August 1, 1939, she made an excited call to her brother. She'd met a friendly man named Frank Martin at a beer joint in Charleston, West Virginia. Martin was not at all shy about spending on her, and inquired if Luther would be interested in a taste of his largesse.

Luther would. In fact, he wanted Martin's whole bankroll. Kathleen propositioned Martin, picked up Luther, and they robbed their passenger of the contents of his wallet.

For this holdup, Luther did not have a gun. He instead pressed a ketchup bottle filled with salt into Martin's back, which he cracked over his head before fleeing in his car. The take from the robbery was thirty-five dollars.

The Maddox siblings were caught within hours, and five-year-old Charlie was taken to the home of his grandmother. The visit was supposed to be for a day or two, but stretched into three, then four, then close to a week. Finally, Family members sat down with the young boy and told him his mother would not be coming back anytime soon. Kathleen had been sentenced to five years in the Moundsville State Prison in West Virginia. Luther received a ten-year sentence.

Manson did not take to the strict religious rules of his grandparents' old Kentucky home any better than his mother did. After a few weeks, the Family decided he would be better raised by his Aunt Glenna and her husband Bill in McMechen, West Virginia. That arrangement had the benefit of being closer to his mother's prison.

Manson would later claim that, as punishment for a minor infraction, his uncle Bill dressed him in girl's clothing for his first day of school. (Others said he had been made to wear a dress after crying at home, an emotion his uncle felt was unmanly.)

Of course, the other kids picked on him until Manson flew into a rage and started fighting everyone. After that, Charlie was permitted to wear boy's clothing.

Charlie's family tolerated his presence—usually by shifting him around to various relatives whenever the Family sheltering him needed a break. In 1943, Kathleen was granted early parole based on her good behavior. Luther, who had made a slipshod escape attempt, would serve his entire ten-year sentence.

If it is ever possible to imagine Charlie Manson truly happy, it would be during the weeks following his mother's release. He loved being with her, and cheerfully joined her when she moved to Charleston, West Virginia. For Kathleen's part,

Charleston meant access to a greater pool of available men. Unfortunately, the presence of a rambunctious, often hostile son would shrink that pool.

Kathleen did manage to find a husband, albeit one whose shared interests started with booze and stopped before including her son. The three moved to Indianapolis, where Kathleen hoped a stable family would give Manson the structure needed to stop acting out. It did not, and tensions between her and her husband grew the more Charlie acted out.

Once again, Kathleen chose the path of her pleasure. She quietly began investigating alternatives to having her son live with her and her husband.

Attempts to place Charlie in foster homes were unsuccessful. In 1947, she enrolled her now twelve-year-old son in the Gibault School for Boys in Terre Haute, Indiana.

At Gibault, a "school for wayward boys" run by Catholic priests, pupils had opportunities for farm work and animal husbandry. Gibault grew vegetables and had livestock, and students were encouraged to take on chores in the fields and stables.

The priests who ran Gibault did want to give the boys who attended an education. And the school was an open campus, a fact the young Manson would avail himself of several times. The strict Catholic atmosphere was particularly unsuited to him, as the only lesson he truly took from the priests was that physical punishment was an appropriate form of discipline. Manson would later use that lesson when wanting to bring people—especially women—to heel.

Manson lasted about a year at Gibault, before making his way back to his mother in Indianapolis. She was not overjoyed to see him, and sent him back.

As Manson would later tell Diane Sawyer in a televised interview, "The only thing my mother taught me was that everything she said was a lie, and I never learned to believe anyone about anything."

Ten months later he fled and started his life of crime. Manson spent a few days breaking into small shops for cash and food. He stole enough money to convince someone to let him have an apartment, despite his young age. But it wasn't long before his petty thievery got him arrested.

Judge Joseph O. Hoffmann, who reviewed his case, was swayed by the tale of woe Manson spun. According to the *Indianapolis News*, Manson said his drunken mother made him leave their home when she entertained men.

Lies tumbled out of Manson easily. He started stealing, he said, when he needed more money to live outside his home. He would not have been caught, except his mother, who wanted him out of the way, let the police know how to catch him.

Manson blended just enough truth with lies to keep his story credible, and the judge recommended he be enrolled in Boys Town, a Catholic-run juvenile care facility in Omaha, Nebraska. The institution was known for its progressive approaches toward juvenile care. Ten years earlier, it had been lauded in *Boys Town*, a 1938 movie with Spencer Tracy and Mickey Rooney. Tracy played a priest who believed there was no such thing as a bad boy.

The first time he heard this line, Manson said: "I think I could be happy working around cows and horses. I like animals."

Manson lasted four days at Boys Town before running away.

This time he had help, and something of a plan. He and another student, Blackie Nielson, stole a car—Manson would later claim it was a hearse. They started driving to Peoria, Illinois, where Blackie had an uncle who was more than willing to train underage boys in the art of burglary.

Blackie and Manson made at least two stops during the 400-mile drive. At one, they robbed a grocery store, and at the other held up a casino. For Manson, at least, these crimes were different from his earlier escapades. The boys had gotten hold of a gun, and for the first time, Charlie Manson had committed armed robbery.

Upon arriving in Peoria, Blackie's uncle welcomed them. The two were successful in their first burglary attempt under the uncle's tutelage, and their $1,500 take netted them $150 from the uncle. Their second attempt was less successful. According to *Peoria Journal Star* columnist Phil Luciano, on March 22, 1949, police received a radio call about a break-in at a Chevrolet dealership. The officers pulled up to a side door at the dealership and waited. As one officer told the paper, a scrawny kid came barreling out the side door and leapt into their car, thinking it was his getaway ride.

Immediately, both officers trained their guns on their passenger, who greeted them with "Ah, shit! Cops!" The kid was Charlie Manson. He had been in Peoria two weeks.

Both Manson and Blackie talked, but they were tied to the two armed robberies committed during their road trip. A return to Boys Town, or some other comparatively cushy institution, was out of the question. This time, Manson was sent to the Indiana Boys School in Plainfield.

The school was much tougher. Many of the boys lodged there had committed serious felonies, and its disciplinarians were free to administer whatever physical punishments they felt necessary. Often, favored boys were allowed to help punish those deemed deserving as well.

At age 13, Manson stood about five feet tall. He was slightly built, and therefore a target for the other boys. Manson would claim he was abused by the staff members, being beaten until he was bloody with a leather strap and raped by bigger boys. He recalled one particularly gruesome episode in which a warden pulled his trousers down in front of other students, picked up raw silage from the floor and spat tobacco juice on it, then shoved it into his ass, laughing that Manson was "lubed up and ready."

During his two years at the Indiana Boys School, Manson attempted to run away multiple times. On October 20, 1949, he was part of the largest breakout in the school's history, when he and six other boys fled.

The boys escaped around seven o'clock in the evening after Manson unlocked an outside door with a stolen master key. They split up after they were off the grounds. Manson stole a car from a nearby farm and the boys drove to Indianapolis.

But he was still the most amateur of criminals and inexperienced in executing crimes and getaways. He was the first escapee caught, nabbed while trying to rob a gas station, less than 24 hours after his escape.

On February 16, 1951, when Manson was 16, he again ran away. This time, his freedom lasted three days. He and two other boys were captured in a stolen car near Beaver, Utah, some 1,600 miles away from Plainfield. During a car search, police found a shotgun in back of the vehicle. Upon questioning, the boys immediately admitted that they had fled the Indiana Boys School and had stolen the gun during a robbery.

Both Manson and another assailant claimed they fled the Indiana Boys School because they had been beaten, with Manson telling the *Indianapolis Star* he had been thrashed "eleven or twelve or thirteen times—I've lost track."

Manson also claimed boys were regularly made to hold down other inmates while they received a beating.

"You have not got much of a choice when they tell you to do it," Manson told the newspaper. "But you'd rather take it yourself than hold them."

Manson would not have a chance to escape from the Indiana Boys School again. Stealing a car and robbing gas stations was one thing. Driving a stolen car across state lines was another. In mid-March 1951, Manson and his two cohorts were sent to the National Training School for Boys in Washington, DC, where they were sentenced to stay until they turned twenty-one.

National Training School was better regulated than Indiana Boys School. While abuses—sexual and otherwise—did occur, they were not as prevalent.

At the school, Manson was given a wide range of psychological and aptitude tests. He was found to have slightly above average intelligence with an IQ of 109 (an average score is 100). However, he had the barest reading skills and was functionally illiterate.

The one subject Manson was truly inspired about was the possibility of being transferred to the Natural Bridge Honor Camp in Virginia. Natural Bridge was a minimum-security facility. Manson was not an ideal candidate for such a transfer, as it was considered a privilege, one given to the most promising, social, and reliable boys. Manson was none of these.

He was, however, manipulative and convinced his psychiatrist his lackluster performance and behavior at National Training School had resulted from his significant inferiority complex, and under his criminal exterior was a funny, sensitive young man who just needed someone to believe in him.

In October 1951, Charlie Manson was given that trust, despite having done little to earn it, and transferred to Natural Bridge. By January 1952, a month before a parole hearing that would have likely seen him released, he was discovered having anal sex with another inmate—while holding a razor to the boy's throat. There would be no parole hearing and Manson was immediately sent to the Federal Reformatory in Petersburg, Virginia.

Manson would later frame the incident as yet another example of his good intentions gone wrong. As he presented it in *Manson in His Own Words*, the other boy was an "undercover queer" who wanted sex, and Manson was willing to oblige. The razor, Manson claimed, was a prop, part of an agreement between the two that would allow the other boy to enjoy the sex yet still claim, if they were caught, Manson had forced him against his will.

Manson immediately reverted to his true nature. During his first seven months at the high-security Federal Reformatory he had racked up a double handful of violations and had been classified as having homosexual and violent impulses. In late September 1952, he was transferred yet again, this time to the Federal Reformatory in Chillicothe, Ohio.

For about a month, Manson rebelled, earning reports that labeled him as needing extensive supervision, and noting his associations with the worst elements at the reformatory.

Then, suddenly, his behavior changed.

While he still chafed under authority, he began taking advantage of the education opportunities at Chillicothe. Within a year he had boosted his reading ability, as well as his math aptitude. He also took a job within the reformatory transportation unit, where he learned how to fix vehicles and generated a good work record.

The reformatory recognized his efforts in January 1954, by presenting him with an award for meritorious service. Four months later, he was given parole. After seven years inside various institutions, at age 19, Charlie Manson was a free man.

Nominally he had been released to the custody of his Aunt Glenna and Uncle Bill in McMechen, West Virginia. But he bounced between their home, his grandmother's house, and even an occasional night at his mother's.

He made at least one stab at normalcy. Despite a reputation as a rough kid, he met, wooed, and won the love of Rosalie Willis, a local girl. The two were married in January 1955. He was 20, she was 17, and they seemed happy.

For a few months, Manson worked a number of legitimate jobs. A few, such as parking lot attendant and service-station attendant, drew on his experience at Chillicothe. But the proximity to vehicles, and his enjoyment of driving, proved a bad combination. He began stealing cars again, eventually commandeering one he would use to drive the now-pregnant Rosalie cross-country to Los Angeles.

His liberty would only last a few months. In October, he was arrested both for stealing the car as well as an earlier offense. As he would later ruefully tell Diane Sawyer, "I wasn't out but a hot second."

However, he had a stroke of luck and, shortly before his twenty-first birthday, a judge gave him probation on one stolen car charge, and he seemed a lock for probation and no jail time on the second. However, he skipped the hearing and headed back to Indianapolis. Once again, Manson was unsuccessful in evading the law. On March 10, 1956, Rosalie gave birth to Charles Manson Jr. Days later, Manson was arrested for violating his probation. He was sent back to Los Angeles, and jail, for three years.

Manson was imprisoned in the Terminal Island facility in San Pedro, California. Rosalie and her son had moved in with Manson's mother, Kathleen, who had moved to Los Angeles. Through 1956, Rosalie made regular visits to Charlie, being the faithful wife in spite of Manson telling a prison psychiatrist he had beaten her, despite loving her.

In early 1957, her visits stopped. Manson's mother informed him Rosalie had moved out of her home and was living with another man. By 1958, she had been granted a divorce and retained custody of Charles Manson Jr. Rosalie remarried, and was on her way to putting that part of her life behind her. Her son would eventually take her husband's name, as well as changing his first: Manson's first child would go through the rest of his life as Jay White.

Rosalie's desertion busted Manson's ego and fuelled his disdain for the straight world. The model prisoner was gone. In his place was left a surly young man who had no interest in the educational or vocational programs available at Terminal Island, save for one.

The prison offered a course based on Dale Carnegie's *How to Win Friends and Influence People*, which codified sales and communication techniques—techniques Manson would soon hone to manipulate others.

Manson charmed officials into letting him enroll. He learned techniques promoted in the book such as: listening to the person you are trying to sell to and reflecting that person's thoughts, being effusive in your gestures, as they help keep the attention of the person you are speaking and not being afraid of giving up credit for ideas.

Manson had other teachers in Terminal Island, carefully listening to the inmates as they talked about theft, burglary, and the thing that caught his attention most of all—pimping.

* * *

If Manson was not striving for early release, he was at least keeping out of trouble. In September 1958, he was paroled, half a year before completing his three-year sentence.

On the surface, Manson worked a series of jobs. He had learned to bartend from one of his fellow inmates. Even so, Charlie was never a man cut out for keeping down a straight job.

"I think the weirdest thing about our relationship was he couldn't understand how I held a job and I couldn't understand how he lived in a cage," says Marlin Marynick, who befriended Manson in the 2000s, visiting him in prison and frequently speaking with him over the phone.

"He tried very hard to explain that to me. He had a real appreciation for the discipline, the uniform. He believed the prison raised him, he believed the guards were in control and accepted them. The whole hierarchy of that system he had an understanding of and he worked within it—sometimes. He would get away with doing whatever he could and he was constantly being disciplined and thrown into solitary confinement."

Charlie took the theories behind pimping he learned and decided to make his income from girls. Using his charm and the persuasive techniques he had picked up inside, he recruited two women. One was a fairly homely woman whose primary allure was her family's wealth, and another was a sixteen-year-old whom Manson turned out to the streets.

Manson had moved in with an inmate buddy but, unfortunately, the man was being monitored by the FBI, who believed he had information regarding a fugitive who had previously lived with him. The feds were not after Manson, but could not help noticing his activities, which they reported to his parole officer.

Manson denied being a pimp, but said he would stop associating with the sixteen-year-old. The other, he said, was fulfilling sexual needs denied to him in prison.

The girl's money, however, was not enough to support him, and on May 1, 1959, Manson attempted to cash a $37.50 US Treasury check he had stolen at Ralph's, a Los Angeles supermarket. Between stealing the check from a mailbox and then forging it, Manson racked up two federal charges.

The charges meant he would be interrogated by Secret Service agents—all of a sudden he was now dealing with a different type of law enforcement. At one point, the main piece of evidence—the check itself—vanished. The agents' best guess was that, while they were distracted, Manson grabbed it and swallowed it.

The case against Manson remained, however, and he accepted a deal. If he pled guilty to forging the check, the mailbox theft portion would be dropped.

Manson seemed headed back to prison, but as the case was being investigated a young woman came forward. She was 19, she said, and was carrying Charlie Manson's baby. The two were in love, and were going to be married. Sending Charlie back to prison would derail not one, but three lives.

The judge who heard Manson's case was charmed, and gave him a ten-year suspended sentence, provided he did not violate probation.

Manson and the girl—actually a prostitute named Leona "Candy" Stevens— immediately went back to their true relationship: pimp and prostitute. She wasn't even pregnant.

The lack of punishment emboldened Manson. He pursued recruiting girls for his stable with new vigor. He also supplemented his income through other activities. In December 1959, he was arrested twice, once for grand theft auto and once for using stolen credit cards. In both cases, miraculously, the charges were dropped due to lack of evidence. Manson must have felt charmed.

His luck appeared to continue. Shortly after his two local arrests, he drove Stevens and another woman across state lines to New Mexico, where the girls were going to turn tricks. He was again arrested and questioned, but released. Once again, he felt untouchable.

Little did he know, the feds had only let Manson go because they needed more time to prepare a case against him.

Either to celebrate his victory or possibly to prevent Stevens from being compelled to testify against him, Manson married his now-legitimately pregnant girlfriend.

The federal case against Manson for bringing women across state lines for the purposes of prostitution was ready by April 1960. Prosecutors only needed one thing: Manson himself. He had abandoned Stevens and vanished to Mexico leaving her willing to testify against him, telling a court Manson had crossed state lines and made her work as a prostitute, to avoid a prison sentence of her own.

While on the run, Manson developed a taste for Mexico. He later recounted stories of mixing with the locals around Mexico City and how he had made a name for himself after approaching a group of local Native Americans and convincing them to give him magic mushrooms.

However, this life didn't last long. The local law enforcement caught wind of the native-befriending gringo, promptly arrested him and sent him back to Laredo, Texas, where he was booked straight into jail.

By June he had been shipped off to Los Angeles. For violating his probation on the check forgery charge, he was sentenced to serve the full ten years which had previously been suspended. The prison system had Manson, and it was going to keep him.

Stevens soon gave birth to a son, Charles Luther Manson, whom Manson likely never met. Both mother and son avoided him, and in 1963—the year The Beatles rose to prominence—Stevens was granted a divorce on the grounds of cruelty and her husband having committed a felony.

Manson served the first five years of his sentence at the United States Penitentiary at McNeil Island, Washington.

While in McNeil Island, he found himself associating with the closest thing he ever had to a father figure, former Public Enemy Number One Alvin "Creepy Karpis" Karpowicz. Manson must have been intrigued by Karpis's rap sheet, which included bank burglary, auto theft, kidnapping, murder, and even train robbery. Karpis had been incarcerated at Alcatraz since 1936, coming to McNeil when the prison was closed in 1962.

At McNeil, Karpis was allowed to play a steel-stringed guitar, drawing on the music he had been raised on during his early years in Kansas. His playing attracted the attention of Charlie Manson, who focused his charm on the hardened con.

Manson—then nicknamed "Tips" by his prison acquaintances—apparently spun his tale of having been brought up in a loveless family situation by a prostitute who at best ignored him. Karpis would later say Manson seemed like a decent enough kid who could use someone doing something nice for him—an attitude that had previously been held by psychiatrists and other authorities. Manson's aptitude for music allowed him to learn quickly from Karpis, who also said he enjoyed Manson's singing voice.

Manson became intrigued, if not obsessed, with the possibility of music stardom. He held a variety of prison jobs, played some sports, and even did a stint with the prison theater group, but his first love became his guitar and songwriting.

By 1964, popular music was shifting and The Beatles played nearly nonstop throughout the prison. Charlie Manson listened—not as a fan, but as someone who understood the influence the band was having. He wanted it for himself—thought, in fact, that he deserved it. Manson had not been able to make pimping and petty crime work for him. Music stardom, however, could offer him everything he ever wanted. All he needed were the right connections.

He found one in Philip Kaufman, who had briefly managed The Flying Burrito Brothers, Gram Parsons's country rock band. After Parsons died of a drug overdose in 1973 at age 26, Kaufman borrowed a hearse, stole Parsons's body, and burned it in Joshua Tree National Park, fulfilling a pact they had made.

He had met Manson while in McNeil prison on a low-level drug charge a few years before.

Kaufman was drawn to Manson's quirky, cool persona. He tells the story of Manson, idling in Terminal Island Prison one day, being called out by a guard, who gleefully informed Manson he was "never getting out of here."

Manson blipped right over the guard. "Out of where, man?" he replied.

Manson's McNeil contacts would spur his music dreams. Creepy Karpis was responsible for bringing the steel guitar to him and Kaufman would, after they both got out, be responsible for producing Manson's only album, *LIE*.

* * *

While Manson himself was only superficially literate, he listened carefully to the utopian visions from a book other prisoners, especially the younger, more tuned-in ones, were discussing: *Stranger in a Strange Land*, the 1961 science fiction novel by Robert Heinlein. The book offered Manson information on two levels. First, it gave him common ground with what younger people, especially those with a bit more education than he had, were reading. The book also served as a touchstone for unfettered sexuality and communal living, as well as introducing the ideas that these behaviors did not have to be considered sinful if done under the auspices of a church. And that church, just as Christianity had been, could easily consist of one leader and a few followers.

More than that, the book illustrated how sexuality could be used as a recruitment tool for such a church.

During this prison stretch Manson also dabbled in Scientology, a system of beliefs rooted in the need to remove the influences of personal trauma. Scientology had been invented by science fiction writer L. Ron Hubbard, who set out to mold himself into an all-encompassing figurehead and leader who was to unquestioningly be obeyed at all times—traits Manson would no doubt have admired. Adherents of Scientology emerge "clear" and assert they are able to see the world as it really is, free of influences that may cloud their ability to analyze.

Manson would eventually claim to be "clear." While he had listed Scientology as something he was exploring in one of his mid-incarceration reviews, by his release in 1967 he was no longer expressing an interest in it. Since Scientology requires participants to invest money in order to advance, Manson would have felt any money he or anyone else had to invest in their spiritual well-being would be better off in his own pocket.

By June 1966, his record was good enough that he was considered for early parole. He was transferred back to Terminal Island, in San Pedro; a first step toward his eventual release, and a prison he felt comfortable in.

That release came on March 21, 1967. But Manson was afraid. Now thirty-three, he had been in reformatories or prison for nearly two decades. The outside world offered him opportunity, but it also represented the unknown. He knew how prisons worked, and how to manipulate people within them.

"There's a story that he begged the warden not to be let out of prison," says Marynick, Manson's pal. "When you get out time goes faster and faster and he couldn't keep up with the pace.

"I asked him about that and he said that was true—he couldn't handle people and the new pace of life.

"When he was in solitary confinement, he told me a lot of it was self-imposed because he couldn't deal with people."

But he was not allowed to stay. Charles Manson had studied Scientology, the murderous Depression-era gangs, the Bible, Dale Carnegie, any number of pimps, and Robert Heinlein.

His hour had come around at last. During the two and a half years until he would be caught and jailed again, he would change the world.

CHAPTER TWO

"These children that come at you with knives, they are your children. You taught them. I didn't teach them. I just tried to help them stand up. Most of the people at the ranch that you call The Family were just people that you did not want, people that were alongside the road, that their parents had kicked them out or they did not want to go to Juvenile Hall. So I did the best I could and I took them up on my garbage dump and I told them this: that in love there is no wrong."

—CHARLES MANSON, COURT STATEMENT, NOVEMBER 19, 1970

Charlie stepped out of prison in 1967 with half-formed delusions of grandeur and was immediately knocked sideways by a world he no longer recognized.

The California before him bore no resemblance to the one of 1959: The clothes, the cars, the talk, the hairstyles had all dramatically changed for the longer and more colorful. However, most painful to Charles was the dramatic change which had occurred in music. He and his guitar style—which he'd been counting on to get work—were a throwback, outdated.

This revelation would have instantly bruised the ego he'd just spent the last seven years building up and probably inspired many flashes of the bitter self-important rages he was known to succumb to.

But, as ever, the first thing on Manson's mind was finding a girl to sleep with him. Luckily he'd just stepped into what was to become the Summer of Love in California and he was headed straight for the heart of it, Haight-Ashbury in San Francisco.

At first Manson set about his vague dreams of becoming a professional musician. He was quickly distracted by the way he was able to persuade young girls to listen to him, sleep with him and care for him, for free—a pattern he would exploit as much as possible for the next two years and would eventually lead him to become a full-on cult leader.

It was a pattern that would continue for the rest of his life, as even from jail his reputation as a murderous madman, half-baked philosophies and defiant nature attracted followers of all ages from around the globe.

"I don't care what decade you're in or what century, there's always going to be a group of souls who gravitate toward these type of people," claims Phil Burton, the father of Afton Burton, the Illinois girl who became the last ever of Charlie's girls, speaking today.

Afton, born in 1989, started corresponding with Manson while still at school. She packed off for California while still a teenager. By 2014 she had carved an X in her head, shaved off her hair, and started calling herself "Star." She lived in the dusty desert town or Corcoran where Manson was imprisoned and visited him as often as she could. She lived in a small apartment on a street where drug deals were conducted openly and worked flipping burgers in a fast food restaurant, hardly a glamorous existence, but one she was prepared to put up with to be near her man. She and Manson were engaged to be married.

"Right after the murders, everybody was in shock and awe and he [Manson] was the devil. And I only think society has evolved to become more and more accepting of darker and darker things," continues Phil.

"Look at the movies and the computer games, that stuff wasn't around in the sixties and seventies. If someone said a cuss word in a movie you freaked out. The blood and the guts, that stuff just pulls something out of people that's already inside. It allows it to manifest in their minds. When they hear about Manson and people like him, there's a huge crowd of people who flock to them—I don't know if it's pity or they're just as unstable as the other guy is.

"I don't know, because I don't have it," he adds.

Afton, with her big hazel eyes, can be seen in many pictures with Manson, by that time in his eighties, gray and withered. In interviews she spoke like the brainwashed girls from the Manson Family of the '60s and refused to explain the root of her attraction to Charles. Her true intentions may never be known, but the marriage license expired and the ceremony never took place.

Before Manson's death Afton had disappeared into the Los Angeles underground, rumored to have shacked up with an artist and model. She surfaced only for Manson's 2017 funeral.

Afton may have been the last Manson girl, but it was in 1967 he met his first.

Manson had stayed with contacts made through prison pals to begin with, wherever he could bum a free night while he hustled on the streets by day.

He later recalled it was around this time he first dropped acid at a Grateful Dead concert and quickly became enamored with the messages of free love and psychedelic-fuelled mind expansion that were spreading across the city—and seized the opportunities they made available to him.

Manson bummed his way from place to place using some of his by-now well-honed techniques for seducing women. The first to become a fully-fledged follower was Mary Theresa Brunner.

Brunner was the polar opposite of Manson and most of the people who ever made it into his orbit. She had made it through college, graduating with a bachelor's degree in history. In 1967, she was twenty-four and working in a library at the University of California's Berkeley campus when she met the shaggy thirty-three-year-old homeless ex-con with a seductive tongue and beady eyes.

Brunner was not especially pretty, but Manson complimented and praised her. In return, she let him sleep at her house and eventually in her bed. While she was not thrilled with having to share him with other women, she put up with it. Over time Brunner was bestowed a number of nicknames and aliases, including "Och," "Marioche," and two that reflected her "first woman" status: "Mother Mary" and "Mary Manson."

Manson was much less than a boyfriend though and would still spend his days on the streets enticing other susceptible girls, and often went for long drives, disappearing for days.

It was from one of those trips Manson returned with Lynette Alice Fromme whom he picked up in the city of Venice in Los Angeles.

Fromme had been born in Santa Monica, California, in 1948 and was a good student at Orville Wright Junior High School. She was a talented dancer, in a troupe that performed at the White House, but developed problems at home and by the time she was thirteen, was no longer speaking to her father. By fifteen she had taken to burning herself with cigarettes and drinking heavily. She then left home permanently after a blow-out fight with her dad.

In 1967, she was drifting when she met Charles. As Fromme recalled in her own autobiography, he introduced himself by telling her people in the area referred to him as "The Gardener," because his role was taking care of "the flower children."

"Don't want out and you're free," he told her, introducing her to the pseudo-Zen statements which made most of his philosophy. "The want ties you up."

Fromme journeyed with Manson first to San Fancisco and then, along with Mary, further north to the Mendocino forest area. There they lived a frugal existence in a shack. Manson continued to develop his 'philosophy' encouraging the girls to free their minds, and encouraging them all to have sex together, so the two girls would lose their inhibitions.

Fromme recounted one instance around this time when she emerged from making love with Manson solo to find Mary sitting on a tree stump and crying. As she described it in her book *Reflexion* Manson only had to say a few words to Mary and suddenly she started to smile.

She added: "I could see that she loved him more than any man in her life, save her father, and maybe even him."

Another time Manson made each girl watch as he had sex with the other. Fromme compared her turn as voyeur to seeing "moving artwork and dance, tenderness and surrender."

The three of them continued to drive throughout the West recruiting other hippies to their merry group, first in a Volkswagen van, and as they attracted more followers, in a black-painted school bus. Because of their status as the first followers, Lynette and Mary were afforded a closer and slightly different relationship with Manson, and were able to assert that authority over the other girls.

A year after they had started on this magical mystery tour with Manson, staying in hippie friendly houses and at roadsides, Brunner gave birth to Manson's son Valentine Michael, the first child born within the Family. He was cared for communally by the group, which by this time had considerably swelled.

Manson was beginning to gain confidence as this ragged band grew. He also realized he needed to include a few male figures, and took on a few eager greasers and burnouts he felt he could get along with—favoring those with mechanical skills who could work on the bus or musicians, whom he could relate to. He also encouraged the girls to share their love and LSD fuelled orgies were not uncommon.

The Family began to hone in on the Los Angeles area and although only loosely knit, they set up a semi-permanent home. Firstly in a communal house in Topanga Canyon known as the Spiral Staircase.

This was one of the few places Charlie claimed legitimately freaked him out, because of the depravity connected with its alternative-living, possibly Satan worshipping inhabitants. After one "Cosmic Gathering" too many, the Family decamped to the basement of a burned out house further up the canyon.

A number of police raids and the lack of amenities forced Charlie and his disciples out, but toward the end of 1968 they found what would become the Family's semi-permanent home in Spahn Ranch, a former movie set and horse-rental stable.

The sprawling 500-acre ranch in the Santa Susana mountains offered Charlie an opportunity to headquarter the group, further refine his philosophies and songs and work on his plan for grabbing the attention of mainstream society—through his music, of course.

Octogenarian ranch owner George Spahn was nearly blind, living at the end of the ranch in a decrepit trailer, and—depending on whom one listens to—he was either charmed or threatened by Charlie. He spent his days tricked out in cowboy duds, although his health prevented him from riding or doing much else.

Aside from George, there were only a few dusty ranch hands to tend to the animals for Charlie to worry about, and he made sure the girls kept them on his side, even though things could become strained—especially as he moved the whole Family in little by little.

Fromme took on the role of looking after George Spahn and the sharp sound she made whenever he stroked her legs inspired her Family nickname: Squeaky. She has always claimed the old man reminded her of a stepfather, playing down various accounts she was his lover.

The ranch itself had its glory days in the fifties and by the time the Manson Family moved in it was crumbling and had barely any amenities. The sets and living quarters later burned down in a 1970 wildfire. A replica of the set was rebuilt by Quentin Tarantino for his 2019 movie *Once Upon A Time In Hollywood*, which featured a fictionalized version of the Manson Family.

As 1968 wore on into 1969 the Manson Family solidified around a core of key members, all of whom assumed their own specific role within the Family. Manson also started to change, grow more confident and develop a certain shamanistic style, often dressing himself in buckskin with leather thongs looped loosely around his neck. He would hold court over meals and monopolized conversations with lectures on philosophy, religion, social injustice, or anything else on his mind. His group listened carefully to his streams of consciousness.

As a former associate of Manson described him, he had developed an animalistic quality, which made him well suited to the desert: "He wasn't as small as I thought he was going to be—and a little more full. I remember thinking he had a reptile-like quality to him, with his skin really tight in places.

"And his eyes you could never escape, they betrayed all of his emotion, and they looked right into you, it could make you shiver. There was something about him—he was one of those people you couldn't take your eyes off, he had a spooky, attractive quality about him."

He would increasingly use these persuasive qualities, doses of LSD and the power he developed over his followers to wreak his revenge on the Hollywood elite who increasingly rejected him, selecting a certain number of them to become his cold-blooded murderers.

One of those figures was Susan Denise Atkins, twenty-one in 1969, who had been the one who originally found Spahn Ranch for the Family to move into.

Atkins had enjoyed a promising start as a member of her church choir and high school's glee club but things fell apart because, she claimed, her parents were alcoholics. Shortly after her mother died in 1963, she quit school and started bouncing around California where she quickly learned how to fend for herself and how to use her looks to get what she wanted.

Atkins met Manson in 1967 and had been a fixture on the scene since. Her long brown hair and cautious smile belied her true nature, which would later lead to prosecuting attorney Stephen Kay to describe her as "the scariest of the Manson girls."

Upon joining the Family, Susan rarely used her birth name, instead going by Manson's nickname, Sadie Mae Glutz, or Sexy Sadie, inspired by The Beatles song of the same title.

The other girls would later claim they never trusted Atkins, that she had a motor-mouth, was always taking off with different guys and telling tall tales. However, she made her way into Manson's inner circle, likely as a result of her predilection for sexy clothes and willingness to follow his orders.

Sadie gave birth to a son in October 1968, with Bruce White, a student at the University of New Mexico who had briefly stayed with the Family. The boy, whom Manson named Zezozose Zadfrack Glutz, was raised communally by the Family.

Later, when Susan was imprisoned for her extremely violent role in eight of the murders attributed to the Family, Zezozose wasn't claimed by any of her family and instead adopted and rechristened. What happened to him after that is unknown.

Another of Manson's closest confidantes was Robert Kenneth "Bobby" Beausoleil, also twenty-one at the time he committed murder.

As a young man in Santa Barbara, California, Beausoleil had been arrested a number of times for running away from home and a series of petty crimes that were later dismissed.

For six years he moved between Los Angeles and San Francisco, but wasn't exactly drifting. Bobby was good looking and talented. He was an actor and played pickup in rock 'n' roll bands, including a forerunner of Arthur Lee's band, Love. Bobby even sang backup on Frank Zappa's *Freak Out* album, though he would later say Zappa did not allow him to officially join his band, The Mothers of Invention, because he did not know how to read music.

Bobby also had a dark side. He had led the Family to the burned out basement in Topanga, and was planning a movie called *Lucifer Rising* (1972). Although he had collaborated with director Kenneth Anger on the film, it was not released until over a decade after he was imprisoned, held back so Beausoleil and other convicts could record its soundtrack behind bars.

Scoring a movie with Lucifer in the title, and his collection of apparently "Satanic" tattoos, did not sit well with review boards during his parole hearings, even though he argued his music had been used in a documentary on Lady Gaga and was therefore valid art.

Despite being recommended for release by the California parole board in January 2019, he remained in prison in August 2019 after state Governor Gavin Newsom reversed the board's decision.

In 1968, Beausoleil had been living with a friend, Gary Hinman, in Topanga Canyon, California. Shortly before the Tate/LaBianca killings that would catapult the Manson Family to popular fascination, Hinman—a small time drug dealer on the side—would became the Family's first victim, and Bobby would be charged with his murder.

Beausoleil also introduced his sixteen-year-old, newly pregnant girlfriend, Kathy "Kitty" Lutesinger, into the Manson Family. Lutesinger clashed with Manson, who generally frowned on his followers having one-to-one relationships. Furthermore, Manson became convinced Lutesinger was trying to pull Beausoleil away from the ranch and the Family. Every once in a while he let her know who was head of the Family and in control by hitting her. She put up with it. So did Beausoleil.

When Beausoleil was arrested in 1969 the Family would refuse to tell Lutesinger where he was. But by the time she gave birth to their child in 1970, she found out, as his murder trial prepared to begin and was splashed across newspapers and the TV.

Lutesinger eventually co-operated with the police and later became a teacher and principal in the Los Angeles school system. Her son has still never known his father as a free man.

Once Bobby was in jail, Charles "Tex" Watson, age twenty-three, became Manson's right hand man.

Watson had gone from an honor student, athlete, and editor of the school newspaper in Copeville, Texas to a jock at the University of North Texas with a bright future. He took advantage of free tickets given to him through his job as a baggage handler at Braniff International Airways and it only took one trip to Los Angeles in 1967 to seduce him to the ways of its rampant drug-and-free-love culture.

Shortly after, Watson left college for California and embraced the hippie scene, working up an enormous appetite for psychedelic mind-bending drugs, which he quickly started selling as a means to support himself.

The drug trade was lucrative enough to allow Watson to buy a car and one day he picked up hitchhiker Dennis Wilson, drummer for the Beach Boys. When he dropped Wilson off at his mansion, he got a glimpse into his incredible world of parties, pools, drugs and girls—most of whom were hangers on staying at his house for the summer. They had come down from Spahn Ranch. Wilson had first become familiar to the Family in late spring 1968, when he picked up Patricia Krenwinkel and Ella Bailey twice in one day. He invited them back to the mansion and they stayed for months—and brought the whole Manson Family with them.

Wilson let Watson stay and he was quickly seduced by the women, and introduced to their mysterious leader, the short, charismatic guitarist they all seemed to idolize. Watson may have embraced the hippie life, but Manson embodied it.

In a book Watson later wrote while in prison, he would describe the Spahn Ranch residents as a couple dozen "mischievous souls." During 1968 and 1969 he began taking more and more drugs and slipping further and further away from straight society.

The solid Texan morals he had been brought up with were eroded; his strong Texan muscles were not. On the night of the Tate/LaBianca killings Watson was by far the most savage and animalistic of the Manson Family murderers, later earning him seven guilty counts of first-degree murder. He remains at the Richard J. Donovan Correctional Facility in San Diego, where he claims to have found God.

Life at Spahn Ranch was very basic with no TV or radio, buckets to use for toilets, few chairs and not even a good electricity line. But somehow Sandra Collins Good was charmed so much by it she gave over her $2,000 trust fund check each month to Charlie.

Most of that wasn't even spent on food, with the Family preferring to go dumpster diving—raiding the garbage cans behind supermarkets and grocery stores where retailers threw away perishing vegetables, too-stale-for-sale rolls and just-past-the-sale-date dairy products. With a little love and careful trimming, they were still edible.

Once the girls even showed up to rummage through piles of discarded food in Dennis Wilson's Rolls Royce, filling its trunk with rotting perishables.

Good remembered her days at the ranch before the murders fondly, and returned there in 2018.

Stoner Van Houten, a local Manson expert who made a name for himself doing tours of the ranch area, met up with her.

He recalled: "I spent five hours with Sandra Good. She said most of the time it was kind of boring. They ate garbage. She described one day she took LSD and went riding a horse, then came back and Charlie was there, and playing music and they just went to the saloon and it was a perfect day."

Shortly before Sharon Tate's life was ended by the Manson Family, they had welcomed the birth of Sandra Good's first child to their fold.

She also recalled the delivery to Stoner, who said: "She didn't have her baby at the ranch. She started to have it in [ranch hand] Randy Parks's trailer and then Tex took her to the hospital and then the next day she stayed back at Spahn one day then went on to Death Valley."

Good was not part of the Tate/LaBianca killings. She and Mary Brunner were in jail at the time for trying to use a stolen credit card.

However, she did end up doing time. In 1976, she and later Family member Susan Murphy sent threatening letters to executives they believed ran corporations which were major polluters. Good received a 15-year sentence and was paroled in 1985.

Stoner added: "She is 75 now, but she still sounds like she did when she was much younger. She's extremely passionate and nice—sometimes you can't get her to shut up!

"She has a grandmotherly instinct, but she is still very much into Manson and the case. She's a huge environmentalist. She's funny and she has loosened up a little bit, but she is very devoted to caring about the air, trees and water."

Two more key members of Manson's entourage were Patricia Krenwinkel and Leslie Van Houten, both teenage runaways from broken homes.

By fifteen, Van Houten was heavily involved in the drug scene in Los Angeles and at 17 she fell pregnant and her mother forced her into a late term abortion. Although she finished school, she left home for Northern California in 1968 and lived in a commune, putting her in Manson's orbit. Soon after meeting him she phoned her family to say she was cutting herself off and that was the last they heard of her—until after the murders.

At the same time Krenwinkle was riding with Manson and his crew in their infamous black bus—so painted after it had been pulled over and cited by police who told them it needed to be changed from yellow to be operated privately.

Krenwinkle—nicknamed, among other things, Big Patty—had met Manson at a house party aged nineteen and been seduced by him that very night. She quickly abandoned her job to travel with his crew.

Both Van Houten and Krenwinkle were later sentenced to death for their part in the Tate/LaBianca murders, convictions later overturned when California briefly abolished the death penalty in 1972. They both remain in prison as of 2019.

Another teenage runaway to join the Manson Family was pretty Ruth Ann Moorehouse. She was first introduced to the budding Family through her father, Dean, who had picked up Charles Manson while he was hitchhiking in 1967. Dean, then a Protestant minister, opened his home to Manson and his two original companions, Brunner and Fromme.

While Manson initially charmed Dean by singing religious songs, he also tried to seduce Ruth Ann and became a frequent visitor to their house. After making it known she was planning to run off with Charles's gang Dean reacted angrily. He hastily married Ruth Ann off, but she soon ditched her new husband and headed straight to Manson.

Dean followed in a bid to get his daughter back, but amazingly, seduced by Charlie, his supply of LSD and the Manson Family lifestyle—he instead became a follower. However, he also became a casualty of the era and would go on to be arrested for a variety of drug and corruption-of-a-minor charges, putting him in and out of prison a number of times before he died in 2010, aged ninety.

Ruth Ann stuck with the Family, and described their life as like "twelve of us apostles and Charlie." She was one of several Manson girls who would maintain the vigil outside of the courthouse during the 1970 murder trial of Charlie and three of the Family, an X cut in her forehead and hair completely shaved.

Ruth Ann's nickname, "Ouisch," was pronounced "Oosh" or "Üsh." While she was not directly involved in any of the Family's murders, she was part of a team of Manson Family members who, during 1970 trials, tried to kill one of the witnesses—fellow Family member Barbara Hoyt, who had previously been a friend of hers.

Hoyt survived their effort, and ended up testifying. Moorehouse fled to Nevada, and while the California district attorney's office issued a bench warrant for her arrest, prosecutors did not feel the expense of bringing her back to face misdemeanor charges was worth the trouble.

Moorehouse has since disassociated with the Family and lives quietly in the Midwest.

A fringe member of the group, but one of its most hard-living members, was Danny DeCarlo. He and his father had sold guns, earning him a place as chief of the Manson Family armory after showing up at Spahn Ranch in March 1969 looking for a place to repair his motorcycle.

However, DeCarlo was primarily the treasurer of the Straight Satans, a vicious outlaw motorcycle gang. Manson had hoped DeCarlo would convince the rest of the Straight Satans to join him at the ranch, so he could use them as a security force to scare off ranch visitors who got overly friendly with his girls, or obnoxious with Family members.

Manson continued to offer goodies to DeCarlo to keep the possibility open.

Not that DeCarlo was in danger of leaving. He made full use of the female resources the Manson Family offered, and apparently had assets of his own—around the Ranch, he was known with some affection as "Donkey Dan."

The Manson Family fluctuated in size between around ten and thirty members while at Spahn and later the Barker ranch. Barker was further upstate and Manson was led there by follower Catherine Gillies, whose family owned a property nearby. Manson was enthralled with the idea of living out in the desert as he felt it afforded more privacy, but his followers were less keen on the harsher desert conditions.

Other members of the Family were problematic, such as Steve "Clem" Grogan. There was an ongoing debate about whether he consciously played stupid or whether he was actually slightly mentally handicapped. The Family would occasionally call him "Scramblehead," and only some meant it affectionately.

In June 1969 Grogan was arrested for exposing himself to young children. He was sent to a hospital for observation for 90 days, but slipped out when one of Manson's girls walked onto the campus and escorted him away.

In 1971, Grogan was convicted for participating in the murder of Donald "Shorty" Shea, a ranch hand at Spahn who had clashed with Manson, which ultimately led to his end. However, his death sentence was commuted to life in prison when Judge James Kolts determined Grogan "was too stupid and too hopped up on drugs to decide anything on his own."

Grogan may have been stupid in many respects, but he was a smart prisoner. While incarcerated, he showed a great deal of remorse, and even drew a map enabling investigators to find Donald Shea's body. It was found, in one piece (as opposed to the nine it had been rumored to be cut into). In part because of his help, Grogan was paroled in 1985, becoming, as of mid-2019, the only Manson Family member to commit murder and leave prison alive.

Seventeen-year-old Barbara Hoyt was another runaway who was only ever half in the group. The Family did not consider her part of its inner circle, and even though she only had a peripheral role in the Tate killings she would eventually turn state's evidence.

Bruce Davis was a part time member of the group. He was a musician and Scientologist. At first he enjoyed the free-flowing sex, later describing the group as "peace and love and music and . . . drugs and sex—just a party."

However, after a stint in London in 1968 he returned to Spahn Ranch to find Charlie and his party had changed significantly. He noted the peace and love vibe was now in the background. In its place was heightened paranoia—against the Black Panthers, the authorities, and the impending collapse of civilization Family members called "Helter Skelter."

Other fringe members of the group included the youngest, Diane Lake, who had been emancipated from her parents at age 14 and lived in the Hog Farm commune, but was driven away by leader Hugh Romney's wife after she had displayed a hyper-sexual nature. Charlie had no problem taking her in.

Catherine "Gypsy" Share was another figure who drifted along with the Family, from around 1967, the same year she made an appearance in the soft porn film *The Ramrodder,* parts of which were filmed at the Spahn Ranch. It was Share who introduced the last member of the Family to join before the killings, Linda Kasabian—little did she know then how she would play a pivotal role in the murders, and later as a witness for the prosecution against Manson.

In 1969 Kasabian was only 20 years old, but had already been married twice—her last name was from her second husband—and become a mother of two. She was only a member of the Manson Family for around two months before she was told to drive the car on August 8, 1969, the night of the five bloody murders at 10005 Cielo Drive. She was reportedly chosen as the only person at Spahn to have a legitimate driving license who was not in jail.

Kasabian stood dumbly by as her cohorts slaughtered five inside the Tate residence that night, later claiming she was paralyzed with fear. At one point she even saw bloody Wojciech Frykowski trying to run away and met his eye. She claimed she said to him "I am so sorry, please make it stop" before Charles Watson found him, stabbed him repeatedly and smashed at his head with a gun butt, killing him.

The next night Manson forced Kasabian to go with the Family on their second night of violence. After leaving three of the Family to kill, Kasabian, Manson and two others drove to Venice Beach. Manson issued instructions for Kasabian to kill an actor named Saladin Nader who was acquainted with the Family and whom she had met a few days previously. However, she sabotaged the plans by knocking on the wrong door and sneaked back to Spahn alone.

Two days later Kasabian fled the ranch for New Hampshire. She wouldn't see any of the members of the Family again—until they were on trial.

CHAPTER THREE

"The power of suggestion is stronger than any conspiracy that you could ever enter into . . . Is it a conspiracy that the music is telling youth to rise against the establishment because the establishment is rapidly destroying things?"
—Charles Manson, court statement, November 19, 1970

Charlie Manson was a con man and a sponge. Throughout his life he sucked up a variety of influences that had been designed to exert power over people. Growing up, he had gone to Christian services, although he had responded to little in them save for the music. In prison he had been exposed to Scientology and Dale Carnegie's *How to Win Friends and Influence People*. On the opposite end of the self-improvement spectrum he constantly listened to pimps' highly embellished stories about keeping stables of women under control. And Tex Watson, who helped kill at least seven people while part of the Family, would later say Manson's talents included mystical skills and sorcery.

Of course, it would not take much to convince a man who spent most of his waking life tripped out on psychedelic drugs of that.

Everything Charlie took in, he retained. It coagulated into a toxic stew of manipulative techniques he could draw from, depending on the circumstances or his target.

In the summer of 1968, before the Family settled at the Spahn Ranch, they were constantly on the move. As the Family traveled, it was exposed to new young people seeking community. There is no record of how many people heard Charlie's philosophies and elected not to join, but they were many. Those that did were attracted by the emotional and physical lures Charlie dangled—he was a spiritual preacher, giving sermons in the religion of Charlie Manson. The Family grew.

Keeping the Family moving was a necessity. Most hosts the Family tapped could carry an ever-growing group of hippie deadbeats for only so long, even if the girls did cook and clean. But Charlie and other Family members seemed to always know one more receptive homeowner. When they did not, Charlie would draw on the goodwill vibe of the Flower Power era, combined with his own personal charm, to convince strangers to give the Family places to rest, whether out of the goodness of their hearts or as a result of whatever services Family members might provide. Charlie was not above letting his girls dabble in prostitution, but in her memoir *Reflexion*, Lynette "Squeaky" Fromme said she and a few of the others' forays into the oldest profession lasted little longer than two nights.

Charlie's on-the-road strategy was well timed, and took the Family away from San Francisco during early 1968. Even then it was a "sanctuary city"—for free living. The hippie scene, which in the mid-1960s was made up of gentle, colorful locals or near-locals, was increasingly being overtaken by burnouts, opportunists, and the mentally ill. Some of these newcomers would eventually make good Family fodder, but the sheer numbers began to turn San Franciscans against the "groovy people."

The constant moving also kept Family members from growing bored or disillusioned; when the Family was exploring new locations, there was no time to reflect.

In the spring of 1968, before moving to the Spahn ranch, Charlie temporarily split the Family. The thinking behind this was his desire to make them long for him. They would return much more grateful and devoted. Some members were sent to stay at a pad in Mendocino, California, while others would later join Charlie in staying at Dennis Wilson's mansion. The Family at this time also had access to the Spiral Staircase House.

Susan Atkins was told to go to Mendocino. This might have been partly in punishment. Atkins, more than other women, would challenge Charlie or attempt to draw attention to herself—definitely not wise in a setting where there could only be one leader.

It also may have been that Manson did not feel confident enough, that the others may start to listen to Susan's challenges and join her in questioning his authority.

Whatever the reason, on June 24, the home where Atkins, along with a handful of other Family members (including Ella Jo Bailey, Mary Brunner, and Patricia Krenwinkel) and local hippies were staying, was raided. The group had been considered a nuisance for a while, but when they were found to be distributing LSD to minors, the community had had enough. The group was rounded up, arrested, and after the media had branded them the "Witches of Mendocino" they returned to Los Angeles.

Susan and the others quickly installed themselves at Dennis Wilson's mansion. When a sexually transmitted infection ripped through the Family and many others crashing there, Atkins was suspected as having introduced it. But Wilson was still willing to let the party continue, even after paying for penicillin treatments as part of what one member of the Beach Boys later described as "the largest gonorrhea bill in history."

Wilson's hospitality would eventually be tapped out in an ugly fashion.

By this time the Family had based themselves more permanently at the Spahn Ranch, primarily in the saloon and jail sets. Sometimes they would sleep in the 20-foot red and white trailer permanently parked near the buildings, and sometimes would just pass out on the musty, moldy, discarded sofas and stuffed chairs that sat in the mud in the middle of what passed for a village square.

Manson, the once-and-future pimp, helped keep the ranch hands on his side. But even then there were limits. Manson would not tolerate any other male playing power games or being rough with his followers and he would chase people away who thought he was running a pay-for-play whorehouse. The reason for that was twofold: he did not want the Family trivialized and did not want law enforcement nosing around.

That said, Manson still used pimp techniques when they suited him. And when there were men Manson wanted to impress, he would trot out what he called his "front-street girls," the prettiest or most sexually alluring, to be readily available to his visitors.

During that first summer and fall at the Spahn Ranch, there was love in the hills outside Los Angeles. Undated movie footage from the ranch shows Family members walking as a group. Their actions do not seem forced, especially when one or two break from the pack and skip ahead. The images are exactly what they should have been during the summer of 1968, while the hippie movement was still strong: a bunch of carefree, colorful young people.

Manson kept his Family members from wondering about other perspectives, whether on the world or their own communal living situation, by keeping them busy. This was a lesson he learned from prison. In addition to the ranch chores, which included looking after the horses, maintaining the stables, and setting up rides at three dollars an hour, there was always cooking, cleaning, and laundry to be done. There was clothing to be sewn and mended. There were cars to steal, cars to maintain—especially Volkswagen Beetles—which he loved to turn into dune buggies. Though those vehicles were not street legal, Manson's plan was for the Family to use them to drive around in the desert. Parts were usually supplied (stolen) by the biker gangs Manson wanted to impress. Occasionally the Family would sell them for a little extra cash.

On some days there would be supply runs, whether for candles—the ranch had little electricity, although it did maintain a phone line—equipment, or food runs, whether through dumpster diving, shoplifting, or the occasional straight purchase. If something was free, Family members would stock up on it. Matchbooks were always popular: Family members frequently grabbed handfuls of them from Ralph's supermarket and other local establishments. They were a key necessity for cigarettes, pot, and cooking.

Sometimes Manson would order one of the girls to sing, sew, cook, or take on a chore she had not done before. If they said they were unable, his stock answer was that if they believed that, then of course they were not able. And then he would push them until they relented.

Manson knew, with some of the damaged souls who had come his way, productive work would give them a stronger sense of self-worth—a sensation within them he had created. And if they wanted more, they had to stay with him. Above all, they were glad to do what they could for him. And he was not above aggrandizing his role. As he would later tell *Rolling Stone* magazine, "People said I was a leader. Here's the kind of leader I was. I made sure the toilets were clean. I made sure the animals were fed. Any sores on the horses? I'd heal them. Anything need fixing? I'd fix it. I was always the one to do everything nobody else wanted to do.

"Pretty soon I'd be sitting on the porch, and I'd think, 'I'll go and do this or that,'" Manson continued. "And one of the girls would say, 'No, let me.' You've got to give up, lie down and die for other people, then they'll do anything for you. When you are willing to become a servant for other people, they want to make you a master.

"In the end, the girls would be just dying to do something for me. I'd ask one of them to make a shirt for me and she would be thrilled because she could do something for me. They'll work twenty-four hours a day if you give them something to do."

In addition to work, there was also much play. The Spahn Ranch offered opportunities for Family members to try on different personas. Sometimes they would be pirates, and sometimes Victorian era settlers in the Old West.

There were other games as well. Sometimes Charlie would get Family members to mirror his actions. He would do this one-on-one, when casually walking by people on the ranch, getting Family members to place their palms against his and track his motions. He would also play it when they were all gathered together, making faces or gestures and expecting the group to mimic him.

It was all a game, Family members thought.

Except it was not.

The subtle message behind Manson's actions was, "I am you, and you are me. You follow me. You do as I do."

Or, as Susan Atkins would later say, "I never questioned what Charlie said. I just did it."

Because, according to the rules of the game, Manson was always the one to be copied. Nobody else would even dream of trying to reverse the roles.

Charles Manson also introduced another, more serious, type of play. As if they were kids going about a game of hide-and-seek, he came up with the Creepy Crawl. This was an exercise in which Family members—alone, in twos, or very occasionally in threes, dressed in all black—would go out at night in a car. They would then slip into people's homes—at that time most people in Los Angeles didn't lock their doors at night. They would then rearrange things just enough to let people know someone had been inside. Thefts were rarely a part of that exercise, it was done as an example to show people how easily and how intimately they could be got at by the Family. This was seen as fun and, on the surface, appeared harmless enough . . . although the confusion and chills it would leave the homeowners was a different matter.

Manson had a few special games that involved dark clothing. He would send Family members—mostly girls—onto the highway dressed entirely in black and they would see if they could stand still when a car approached. The object of the game was to conquer one kind of fear.

Manson watched these games carefully to see who responded well. Even though it was presented as a defensive tactic, something which built survival skills, he had plans for those who embraced it best and participated most willingly.

Sometimes idle Family members, especially more presentable ones, were sent out to Los Angeles to panhandle. Those whose charms were not as apparent might occasionally write a bad check or two. The Family was always on the lookout for credit cards they could snatch and use quickly, before their theft had been reported.

It's hard to know whether readily available sex or enlightenment were more powerful lures. Charlie used both very effectively.

Dianne Lake had been treated diffidently by her parents—by her own admission, they were not "the warm, fuzzy, hugging variety"—under the guise of giving her freedom. Her sense of rejection had been heightened by being thrown out of her previous commune for her sexual activity as a fourteen-year-old.

Charlie likely coaxed Lake's frustrations and desires out of her when she sought permission to join his Family. As Lake tells it, she walked in and heard two girls, doubtlessly prompted by Charlie, scream with joy at her arrival. She would later describe that arrival moment as magical, and feeling as though her presence in the Family was meant to be.

Charlie himself initially expressed love and adoration for her. The more she responded to his words, the more he laid it on, reading her cues and furthering the high she was feeling. As Lake later realized, part of the reason she stayed with the Family was to experience the high of his love.

But Charlie was too crafty to fulfill Lake's every need. Doing so would have empowered her, and Charlie did not want his followers to be overly empowered. Lake sought sexual contact, especially with Charlie, the father figure, and she let him know.

Early during her time with the Family, Lake propositioned Charlie, and the two walked to a small hideaway, which initially excited Lake.

However, Charlie then forced her to have anal sex with him. It was sexual contact, but not tender and certainly not caring.

This, Charlie told her when he was finished, was the way sex was given in prison. A lesser partner does not ask a dominant partner for sex. While Lake would have sex in abundance during her time with the Family, she would never again approach Charlie. But Charlie's love was separate from sex, and she continued to receive it . . . or so she thought.

Charlie flipped the playbook for men, using freely available sex to lure them. Sometime Family member Paul Watkins was recruited this way.

In early 1968, Watkins had participated in an orgy with Charlie and a few of his female followers. It was a delicious experience, but also a one-off. Watkins moved on from the crew without having any emotional residue from the experience. The hippie world was small enough, however, that another meeting would be likely. On July 4, 1968, Watkins was picked up on a Los Angeles street corner by two of the women he had had sex with at the orgy. They flirted heavily and he was more than happy to be driven to the Family's new base at the Spahn Ranch.

Watkins arrived with the two girls and was led to the rest of the group, who were splayed out in one of the ranch's buildings. At the door, he was met by two more pretty girls—Lake and Nancy Pitman. He was also greeted by a large wave of marijuana smoke, which did not displease him at all.

From inside the building came Charlie's voice: "Invite him in."

Watkins was received with a wealth of compliments from the women inside, which he happily reciprocated. He also reciprocated Lake and Pitman's offer to have sex with them.

During a rest moment, Charlie took Watkins aside and confided in him. He gestured at the nude women adorning the room and said, "They're yours." As

Charlie put it, he was alone with the women, and would welcome help keeping them satisfied.

Intrigued, Watkins told Charlie he would remain with the Family for the remainder of the summer. He ended up staying well beyond.

These were not the only ways Charlie used sex to indoctrinate or tame his followers. Manson had a curious way with his women. Early in the Family's development, when it was just Charlie, Fromme and Brunner, he suggested that the three marry each other, even though doing so was illegal. The mere suggestion was enough to offer the needy Fromme the taste of support and intimacy she craved. Through the force of her personality, humor, energy, and absolute devotion to Charlie, she would be treated as Charlie's second-in-command.

Charlie consistently preached his sex, love, and brotherhood gospel through 1968. Doing so made sense, as it brought in followers and kept the Family together. But Charlie also realized the power of making his followers accept non-mainstream sexual practices.

Male Family were allowed to freely indulge in their female compatriots, and vice versa. But eventually males and females were required to overcome any sexual hang-ups they might have, whether same-sex couplings, distaste for threesomes, foursomes, or other configurations of random male/female ratios, sexual practices, or anything else that might be an inhibition.

Occasionally, during the first time Charlie had sex with one of his girls, he would ask them whether they had ever had fantasies about their fathers. Many had come from broken or abusive homes, and fantasies about gaining their fathers' acceptance or love often took the form of sexual fantasies. Charlie's guess was a fairly safe bet.

To girls who had come from either religious or repressed homes, Charlie's question would likely seem a revelation. Somehow, this man with the piercing eyes knew their most private fantasies . . . and he was encouraging them to safely act on them with him. A formerly lost girl who had found a family was not going to leave a man like that.

Charlie was perfectly able to flip this scenario when it suited him. When Dean Moorehouse tried reclaim his teenage daughter Ruth Ann from the group, Charlie stopped him in his tracks with the line "You're just angry because you want to do to your daughter what I'm doing," according to a 1970 profile in the *New York Times*.

Manson then turned every bit of charm and persuasion he had onto Dean, including kneeling and kissing the preacher's feet, helping to convert him to his twisted way of thinking.

Real parents presented a threat to Manson. No matter how angry Family members may have been before they joined, there was always the possibility they would have a longing for home. Manson tried to short-circuit that impulse through his teachings.

"He would show us how our parents had not raised us right and had abused us, had tried to shut down the light we had within," said Catherine Share.

If there was going to be any rejection or emotional manipulation, it was going to be done by Charlie. And sometimes that meant not giving it a chance to flourish on its own. To break down the trappings of resentment and jealousy, he would decide who would fuck whom during the orgies. Nobody would refuse, and nobody would feel rejected.

Everyone was free to have sex, but anything that smacked of exclusion or a potential power bloc which might threaten Charlie's authority, such as a monogamous pairing, he attempted to sabotage.

There's no record of where he might have learned such techniques, but Paul Watkins described pre-orgy exercises that have a strong resemblance to tantric sex. Manson would have participants lie on the floor and take deep breaths, and then slowly start to touch each other.

Sex was more than a bonding experience. It was a way for Charlie to gauge whether new Family members would buy into the group dynamic. Sherry Ann Cooper, a.k.a. Ruth Ann Heuvelhorst, was a fringe Family member. In a 1970 interview, she said Charlie never really trusted her because she refused to participate in orgies.

Decades later, Manson would later demonstrate the rules, and the impact, of the Family's sexual mores to *Rolling Stone* journalist Erik Hedegaard. Charlie placed his hand on Hedegaard's arm and moved it up to his elbow.

"This is what it was like," Charlie said. "We all went with that. There's no saying no. If I slide up, you've got to go with the flow."

According to Hedegaard, going with the flow felt "unexpectedly good," although he acknowledged that someone close enough to touch someone else is also close enough to kill that person. Charlie doubtless knew that, too.

Manson had other methods beyond sex for controlling groups. There was a communal clothing pile. This was another idea geared toward breaking down individuality. If there was no ownership, there would be no jealousy. Anyone who liked a specific dress would have only to wait a day or two before having a chance to wear it. Of course, Family members were free not to wear clothing at all if they chose.

Most of the clothing was colorful and relatively clean—laundry was a daily task. But as 1969 wore on, more and more black items, such as one might want when seeking the cover of night, began making their way into the mix.

Even toothbrushes were considered communal property. Need one? Take one. When people are free to have sex with all their brothers and sisters, a personal, private toothbrush was a selfish indulgence.

Newspapers, radios, and televisions, which could bring disturbing news of the outside world—or even worse, news that might contradict the vision of society Charlie would weave for his flock—were limited. Even Family members who needed eyeglasses gave them up: Charlie said glasses prevented people from seeing the world as it really was.

A Manson girl could wash clothes, cook, and clean without glasses. But it would be harder for her to gather information which might prove detrimental to Charlie. However, rather than issue an outright ban, he wrapped what was effectively a ban in a pseudo-mystic philosophy. Family members happily surrendered their glasses.

Sex and emotional dependency worked well for Manson. But if what he wanted was true submission, he was going to have to move beyond those techniques.

Within the Family, drugs were readily available. Manson would cheerfully provide his girls to visiting dealers to maintain his stash. But for Charlie, drugs offered another means of control, dulling the abilities of his followers to think for themselves.

As Tex Watson, the sole male to participate in the Tate/LaBianca murders would later write, "The drugs we all took together and the lack of sleep . . . made us extremely open to suggestions, and the force of a stronger personality."

Manson, in his role as spiritual leader, also delivered a constant stream of sermons. Sometimes they would be on crowd-pleasing subjects such as free love, or the joys of expanding one's mind through drugs, or the beauty of the commune as family. He would talk about the need to give up the material things of the world, the things that turned people into "pigs."

He would return to this topic often, especially when Family members needed a little extra encouragement to turn their allowances, trust funds, or other possessions over to Manson—for the good of the Family, of course.

There were lectures on Manson's childhood experiences, all filtered to portray him either as an object worth pitying, or respecting, or admiring. His petty crimes, when he discussed them, would turn into revolutionary acts.

Sometimes there may even have been occasional truths in those discourses.

Much later, Manson would claim he saw a clear distinction between when he had to tell the truth and when he could lie. Prisons, he said, were places where truth was necessary.

"If you lie, you get punched," he told Diane Sawyer in 1993. "There's a certain amount of truth in prison, and being raised in prison I was pretty much raised in the light of that truth."

On his best days, Manson was an unreliable narrator, and it's hard to see him telling the truth in prison. What stands out is the distinction he drew. If prisons were places where truth was necessary, the world outside did not have such a restriction.

Of course, one must never laugh at Charlie Manson. Patricia Krenwinkel recalled laughing at him once, and he grabbed her by the hair and threw her against a wall. It was not done playfully.

Manson would also hand around the day's drugs in a Christ-like manner, a perversion of the Bible passage Matthew 26:26:

While they were eating, Jesus took bread, and when he had given thanks, he broke it and gave it to his disciples, saying, "Take and eat; this is my body."

For the most part, these drugs included those that provided a good mellow, such as marijuana. But other drugs, such as hashish, belladonna, psilocybin, mescaline, and opium would occasionally float through the camp.

It was only years later that several Family members realized Manson always seemed more in control, as he had been taking less than the others. At the time it did not seem like a big deal. More for everyone else.

Of course, the rampant drug use took its toll, particularly on Watson, who has claimed he was high for days at a time. In another example, without the structure of outside life, Leslie Van Houten's appetite for drugs was limited only by their availability. By her own admission she became "saturated in acid," unable to relate to anyone who was not immersed in psychedelic culture.

Manson understood the power of music, but banned radio use by the Family, although ranch owner George Spahn was free to listen to country music on his own set. The Family girls who served as Spahn's aides believed being allowed to enjoy Spahn's radio was a sign of how much Manson trusted them. Lynette Fromme, Spahn's main handmaiden, must have considered it a reflection of her second-in-command position within the Family.

Unspoken was the fact that Manson's gifts for manipulation meant a small handful of Family members would each, when interviewed, refer to themselves as his second in command.

At the ranches only a few albums were allowed, such as the Moody Blues, The Beatles, and of course Manson's own music. The Family members embraced Charlie's music as eagerly as any Top 40 record, but despite its winning some interest from producers, they were more interested in the figure of Manson and how he presented himself. The music he made was seen as average at best and by no means good enough to make it into the charts. Producers encouraged him to play up his jail persona, but Charles refused, instead concentrating on songs that would further his self-developed "philosophy."

Manson would often use music to charm potential initiates, or to guide the thinking of Family members. Sometimes he would assure those who felt they had no musical ability that they could play or sing if they just tried. They were usually gratified if they did—once Manson said someone could sing or play, nobody was going to disagree.

His own song lyrics were usually straightforward suggestions or requests regarding how he wanted people to behave, such as urging women to surrender and serve men. He was also a huge believer in the power of the stream-of-consciousness and would make up lyrics on the spot which would remind Family members of what had driven them to him, such as their anger toward their parents.

Other compositions were a little more obvious and direct—Tex Watson recalled one song with the refrain "Close the bathroom door, stupid."

One of the more striking examples of this are the lyrics of "Cease to Exist," which became a Manson anthem (and, later, a major bone of contention between Manson and Beach Boys drummer Dennis Wilson):

Pretty girl, pretty, pretty, pretty girl

Cease to exist

Just come and say you love me

Give up your world

. . .

Submission is a gift

Go on, give it to your brother

Manson had been calling himself Charles Willis Manson, taking the middle name from his first wife, since July 1967. It was another sound-good item that could be interpreted in a number of ways, all of which were flattering. His will was of mankind's will. His will was the will of the son of man.

When the Family was in a drugged and susceptible state, Manson would sometimes re-enact the crucifixion of Jesus Christ—taking the title role, of course. And like Jesus, he would proclaim his love for his Family, and his willingness to die for them. Since he would die for them, would they die for him?

That was a pretty heavy trip, especially for those who had come to Manson with a Christian upbringing. Was Manson the resurrection of Jesus Christ? He was not shy about drawing comparisons.

"He'd say, 'I-I know I died on the cross before,'" Van Houten told her court-appointed attorney Marvin Part.

"He told about a suicide-dream sort of, like an acid trip he had one time . . . when he first got out" of prison in 1967.

Van Houten recalled similar lectures—the constant diatribes meant there would be a fair amount of repetition, and repetition meant programming. Although, "he said that all of a sudden he was . . . carrying the cross again, and he was being nailed on it. And Mary, the first girl that was ever with him, was crying at his feet . . . if you could give up your personality and your ego and be willing to die, then you were already dead . . . the body didn't mean anything."

It was a lucky break for Manson that the first girl he pulled into the Family was named Mary [Brunner]. And Manson being Manson, he made the most of it.

Regardless, Van Houten was already convinced.

"I believe that he's Christ. I would never deny it," she would say after being arrested for the LaBianca murders.

Paul Watkins remembers Manson making similar claims, describing how "he had been hanging on the cross for 2,000 years and it did not do a damned bit of good, so now he was up again."

The privilege of Jesus's death may have been reserved for Manson, but he had other deaths in mind for his followers. Manson would often speak of the death of the ego, the death of the self, as a necessary step to achieve a transcendent life. The phrasing of a metaphoric death also reinforced the idea of willing to experience a physical death—which, when Family members went into dangerous situations on his behalf, would hopefully reduce or eliminate their fear.

Sometimes the lessons around death were more practical—and violent. About a month after Paul Watkins joined the Family, Manson attacked him, choking him. Watkins knew he could not fight back. There were too many Manson followers around.

Watkins had heard enough of Manson's philosophy to know this was some sort of test. That said, failing it would have been fatal. Manson, Watkins felt, would have choked him to death.

So Watkins used the only defense tactic he could. He surrendered. He accepted his own death. And the moment he did, Manson removed his hands from around Watkins's throat.

Most of the time, physical lessons were not necessary. When Manson attempted to quash Family members' egos, he would also blend powerful forces from their upbringing into his programming efforts. According to Krenwinkel, when Family members wanted to point out hang-ups and inhibitions in others, the phrase most often used was, "I can see your mother on you. It's still the conditioning. You haven't gotten rid of it.

"You're not dead yet."

Family members would celebrate "ego death" as a stage in their personal evolutions. Paul Watkins said that during group acid trips, Manson would start talking about death, leading Family members to experience it in a hallucinogenic-inspired way. Once they had died and been reborn, they would be willing to give up essential elements of their identity, such as their survival instincts and their names.

Later, after his arrest, Manson would discuss death with *Rolling Stone* magazine, giving reporters a taste of some of the rap he would lay on the Family.

"The death trip is something they pick up from their parents, mama and papa. They don't have to die. You can live forever. It's all been put in your head.

"They program him by withholding love. They make him into a mechanical toy. Children function on a purely spontaneous level. Their parents make them rigid. You're born with natural instincts and the first thing they want to do is lay all their thoughts on you. By the time you're nine or ten, you're exactly what they want. A free soul trapped in a cage, taught to die."

Of course, there was at least one pure mind within the Manson Family. As Barbara Hoyt said, "Everyone considered Charlie a pure soul. He had only managed to go through a few years of school, so he was not programmed with society's rules and laws. . . . He wanted us to discard our upbringings, our knowledge, and our hang-ups and live in the now."

While Manson always promoted growth through recruitment, childbearing was an encouraged means of bringing new minds into the Family. At one point in 1969, the Family boasted more than a half dozen children among its ranks. The first was Valentine Michael Manson, whom Manson sired with Mary Brunner. Manson named his son after Valentine Michael Smith, the protagonist in *Stranger in a Strange Land*.

Valentine would later go on to become one of the only children of the Manson Family to lead a somewhat normal life. He was raised by his maternal grandparents, who re-named him Michael Brunner. In his only print profile, written in 1989 when he was twenty-one, *Star* magazine described how "[a]mazingly, the child whose sole inheritance was a name synonymous with hate, has grown up to be a decent, well-adjusted young man now living in a small Midwestern town.

"A lanky blond with a Rod Stewart haircut, Michael is spending his summer cruising in his 1984 black Pontiac Fiero, hanging out with friends, fishing and tubing down the river."

In the accompanying interview he said how: "I don't feel as if I have to do good because of [Manson]. I try to do good things anyway.

"I don't consider him my father. I have no desire to see him. He's just some evil person somewhere far, far away.

"I never got into fights with kids about whose dad is bigger. What am I going to say? My dad can kill your dad when he's asleep?"

Brunner also described his mother as "more like a special sister," and said he saw her often.

The second child born to the commune was Susan Atkins's boy Zezozose Zadfrack, in October 1968. By late 1969, Sandy Good would give birth to her son, Ivan Pugh.

Manson would claim that a baby's mind was the perfect state of consciousness. Of course, as Family members strove to emulate the unfettered mind of a newborn, it left plenty of room for Charlie to fill their brains with his own philosophies. As one marginal Family member recalled, Charlie was fond of saying that providing children with LSD was no less moral than sending them to military school. Against the backdrop of the Vietnam War, this resonated—and cleared the consciences of Family members who gave or sold drugs to kids.

In 1969, the dominant impulse of the Manson Family shifted from love to fear. And it was more than just the armed guards Manson had taken to posting around the ranch, as much to keep Family members in as intruders out.

On December 31, 1968, Manson gathered the Family around a bonfire at a satellite location—the Myers Ranch in Death Valley, California. It was here Charlie laid out a grandiose scheme for the Family's role in an upcoming race war, where black people would rise, whites would be caught off guard, resist valiantly, but eventually be defeated.

The signs were everywhere, from the racially charged 1965 Watts riots in Los Angeles to the 1967 Detroit riot and the 1969 York riot in Pennsylvania. Then there was the assassination of Dr. Martin Luther King that same year and the rise of the militant Black Panther Party.

The race war could be seen only by those truly tuned into the *zeitgeist*, the mood of the world at a particular time. The Beatles were four such tuned-in people. While it was rumored they had been coding messages in some of their earlier work, in their self-titled record usually referred to as The White Album they were drawing attention to the upcoming conflagration, Charlie thought.

The White Album, Manson said, identified the problem. It counseled those who could hear the messages as to what was "coming down fast."

According to Manson, there was proof a-plenty in The White Album, not only that Helter Skelter was coming, but that Charlie Manson was specifically being called to lead those who would survive. Manson would sermonize on Helter Skelter constantly, revealing the clues he claimed to hear in its songs. For instance, according to Manson's interpretation:

* "Blackbird," with its refrain demanding the blackbird to rise, was a call to black militant action.
* "Don't Pass Me By" and "I Will" were some of many calls from The Beatles to Manson in which The Beatles were seeking a musician to serve as their spiritual leader.
* "Happiness is a Warm Gun" reiterated the need for blacks to arm and defend themselves.
* "Helter Skelter" not only gave the coming race war its name, it set a timetable—per the song, it was "coming down fast." However, according to Beatle Paul McCartney, the song was about a slide-like ride at an amusement park.

* "Honey Pie," a song about transatlantic yearning, was a call for Manson to join The Beatles, either physically or in their call for the uprising, and record a follow-up album. If the White Album was a description of the carnage to come, Manson's album was to offer a blueprint for survival. The Family would make several attempts to contact The Beatles and start a dialog. These were all ignored.

* "Piggies" was a shot at the pigs in the decadent white upper class, which was so devoted to feeding their own appetites they would even indulge in cannibalism, eating bacon. The song suggested this class needed "a damn good whacking."

* "Revolution 1" was a flat-out call for the uprising. While there was a line about The Beatles wanting to be counted out if there was destruction, the line is immediately negated by "in" being sung. Manson interpreted this as meaning The Beatles had been on the fence about violence, but were now embracing it.

* "Revolution 9" was an audial collage that included gunfire, screams, news reports, babies, and heavenly choirs. It, along with Revolution 1, were winks at the apocalypse-studded Book of Revelation.

* "Rocky Raccoon" reinforced the ideas in Blackbird about black uprising, with Manson indicating the "coon" in the name of the hero of the song having a "revival" was a not-so-subtle—and definitely racist—indicator of a black uprising. Manson saw no contradiction in this. At his core, he believed blacks were inferior to whites—an observation not necessarily agreed with by some of his followers, including Lynette Fromme.

All of this was mixed in with a more traditional end-of-times Christian theory. The Book of Revelation was especially useful to Manson. In Revelation 9:2, a fifth angel—The Beatles being the first four—was given a key to a bottomless pit. Revelation 9:4 describes how locusts "were told not to harm the grass of the earth or any green plant or any tree, but only those people who do not have the seal of God on their foreheads." Manson claimed he knew what this seal looked like, and would reveal it in time.

Where would the Family fit into all this? By hiding in the desert, waiting out the carnage, by not being taken by surprise, Family members would be best suited to survive. And when they did, they would emerge from the desert to a destroyed world, one in which black people, having wrested power from their white oppressors, would find themselves lacking the organizational skills to create the world anew, and turn to enlightened white governors to lead them. Those governors would be headed by Charlie Manson and his followers.

"I totally believed Charlie," Share later said. "I believed that the cities were going to burn. I believed my only safety was to stay with the Family. I believed Charlie knew best."

So did others. Leslie Van Houten would later tell one of her lawyers that "a couple hundred thousand people"—Manson likely said 144,000, a number that plays often in Biblical numerology, especially end-of-times predictions—would end up in the center of the earth and stay there for fifty years.

"We wouldn't be old, because we wouldn't age," Van Houten said. "Because to go into the hole, you would have to be perfect in your mind and your body."

Water would be supplied by a branch of the Armargosa River. As some Family members would claim, there was already a civilization down there, waiting for the Manson Family to join them.

Long after his trials were over, Charlie would assert that the entire Helter Skelter scenario was an invention by prosecutor Vincent Bugliosi to tie all Family crimes to him. But the outpouring of scattered details from myriad Family members, along with the allegations that Charlie had done his first rap on Helter Skelter on New Year's Eve 1968, indicate it was a very real thing and many months in the brewing, chewed over by all of the other Family members.

Charlie did his best to make his followers believe in Helter Skelter, no matter how implausible it may be—now they just had to find a way to trigger it.

CHAPTER FOUR

"I live in my world, and I am my own king in my world, whether it be a garbage dump or if it be in the desert or wherever it be. I am my own human being."
—CHARLES MANSON, COURT STATEMENT, NOVEMBER 19, 1970

Outside of the Family, people did not view Charlie Manson as the messianic figure he saw every day in the mirror. Between the summer of 1968 and the fall of 1969, three people successfully challenged Manson's infallibility. One stood his ground and came off relatively unscathed, one experienced the scare of a lifetime, and one would not survive.

Manson lacked self-perspective. One of the cornerstones of a messiah complex is that even if an individual does not believe he or she is a messiah, they are destined to become one. They are not just part of a movement, they *are* the movement. Adolf Hitler is the gold standard of this disorder. Manson was not far behind in dementia, if not in numbers killed.

Manson's omnipotent view of himself carried over to his assessment of his musical talents. By most accounts, Manson was only slightly better a musician than he was a criminal. Nonetheless, he brought drive, shamelessness, and sociopathy to his quest. His adoring bevy of women and manipulation tactics got him into the orbits of recording industry luminaries. But his talent could not keep him there. Rather than recognize his own limitations, he shifted blame and rose to anger.

In time, one of the most prominent targets of Manson's wrath would become record producer Terry Melcher.

Manson's hate for Melcher—son of screen legend Doris Day—was born out of his runaway ego. Manson was sure fate had put Melcher in his path for the purpose of creating a masterpiece album. Manson felt in his head he was destined to become a rock star bigger than The Beatles—yet better, because he would be the one to unite the children, and his message and philosophy would inspire teens all across the western world. He would be the one to bring about a "new consciousness" and enlightenment. In his mind, he felt he was capable of this, not realizing the huge gap between the confused misfits he had convinced to join him and the rest of society.

He was so assured he felt nobody could say no to Charlie.

Eventually, Melcher would. But not at first.

When Dennis Wilson first picked up Patricia Krenwinkle and Ella Bailey in 1968 and took them to his house he must have been delighted at the thought of two young, free loving hippie women at his Sunset Boulevard mansion. However, they spent hours talking about how great and life changing Charlie was. Ever the optimist, Wilson let them stay at the home while he went to a nighttime recording session.

Wilson arrived home at 3 a.m. to find Charlie Manson himself standing at his back door. Manson welcomed Wilson into his own home by dropping to his knees and kissing his feet—a tactic he had used to disarm people before.

Walking into the house, Wilson found himself face-to-face with Krenwinkel, Bailey, and a dozen more Family members whom they had invited, nearly all of whom were female.

Manson easily won Wilson over. They bonded over music and girls, and Manson's ability to say what others wanted to hear convinced Wilson he had found a spiritual leader, someone through whom he could achieve a certain level of enlightenment.

Furthermore, the girls were more than willing to cook, clean . . . or do anything else the men at the mansion wanted.

The Manson Family took, and took a great deal. The number of uninvited guests soon doubled. Members happily indulged in drugs on Wilson's tab, helped themselves to items around the homestead, and took Wilson's clothing, credit cards, and cars as desired.

Wilson enjoyed the idea of an on-call, on-premises spiritual leader. Manson drew on his Dale Carnegie teachings—tell people what they want to hear, be enthusiastic in your presentations, build up your listener—as well as his mix of spiritual and hedonistic philosophies, and fed them to Wilson.

In return, Wilson indulged Manson's musical grandiosity. He and Manson jammed together, and made a few attempts at collaboration. He arranged for recording time in a Santa Monica, California, studio (which did not end well because Manson refused to take suggestions from people in the control booth). He introduced Manson to a variety of Hollywood stars and children of stars, including Rudi Altobelli, who managed some of the entertainment industry's top talent, and producer Terry Melcher.

Melcher was born into the celebrity lifestyle because of his mother, but at age twenty-six, in the summer of 1968, he was established in his own right. He shone as a television and record producer, orchestrating hits for Paul Revere and the Raiders, the Byrds, and other chart-topping California acts.

Melcher had been a longtime friend of Wilson and stopped by the ongoing party at his mansion. That's where he first met Manson, who was surrounded by half a dozen people, playing his guitar and singing.

Wilson had been enthusiastic about Manson's music, although whether it was real or just playing to his ego seemed like the best way to keep the party going was not clear. At any rate, musician Manson was introduced to hitmaker Melcher.

Manson was clearly the more impressed of the two. Melcher did not hear anything exceptional in those first songs, but he also knew that a casual gathering, where the performers had not been in audition mode, more than likely was not the best setting to properly evaluate talent.

Melcher eventually bummed a ride from Wilson; somehow Manson managed to tag along, sitting in the back seat as the Beach Boys drummer drove his friend home.

Manson, Melcher, and Wilson drove to a quiet part of Benedict Canyon, north and west of Beverly Hills. They drove through a gate, behind which was a 4,600-square foot French country-style estate with a small guest house in the back.

Manson and Wilson stayed in the car. Melcher got out, and went to the home he had been renting, along with his girlfriend actress Candice Bergen, since the summer of 1966. The house was part of an estate at 10050 Cielo Drive—an address that would loom large in many people's lives by year's end.

Melcher might have forgotten Manson then and there, but neither Wilson nor his protégé were going to let him. Wilson still saw himself as a springboard for his guru's career. And Manson saw music stardom and his golden opportunity to be bigger than The Beatles.

Melcher was ultimately more interested in Ruth Ann Moorehouse, one of the prettiest of Manson's girls. By one account, he wanted her to move into the home he shared with Bergen and serve—nominally—as their housecleaner. Bergen put her foot down on that plan, and with that Manson, whose musical abilities were those of a talented amateur, had little left to offer Melcher.

Wilson still believed in Manson, however, and arranged studio time for him. But Manson still refused to take any direction from producers during the sessions and the recordings were deemed unusable. What percentage was the artist and how much was the messiah complex is difficult to say; rock-and-rollers were notoriously fussy about their personal expression and frequently acted in an entitled manner. With Manson, it was undoubtedly a schizophrenic partnership between the artist and the violent enforcer. At one point, Manson pulled a knife on the head engineer, and after two days the recording sessions had come to an end.

Manson did not see this as a result of his over-the-top antics. He thought it meant there was enough material for an album. The importance of that belief cannot be understated. In an era before any wannabe recording artist could capture a tune on a smartphone and drop it on any number of platforms, a performer needed vinyl—either a two-sided single or an LP. Having even a small label release your work was a coup. For a major label to release your album, was almost guaranteed stardom.

Manson, of course, would have had an across-the-board belief in his miraculous destiny.

Wilson, however, had a different view. He reviewed the tapes as potential source material for his own contribution to the next Beach Boys album. One tune, "Cease to Exist," had some promise. To Manson, that sounded an awful lot like a co-writing credit for a song released on a major label . . . which Wilson was happy to let his spiritual advisor believe.

Meanwhile, several members of the Family were living well and without restrictions at Wilson's mansion. However, after several costly and destructive months, including an incident in which Clem Grogan stole—and wrecked—Wilson's uninsured Ferrari, Wilson's manager evicted the group, which decamped to the Spahn Ranch.

There are several stories regarding why Manson and Wilson went their separate ways. According to one, someone realized several of the girls who hung out with Manson at Wilson's mansion were underage.

In another, Wilson supposedly saw Manson kill a black man and stuff him into a well. However, no such murder was ever reported.

Another has several different versions, with Manson threatening Wilson by either pointing a gun at him, showing him a bullet, or leaving a bullet in Wilson's bed.

The most likely, however, is that with the end of his rental agreement on the mansion coming up, Wilson fled, leaving his manager to tell the Family it no longer had a place to crash in the ritzy part of Los Angeles. Despite kicking them out, Wilson remained on friendly terms with the Family. That would change.

By some reckonings, the expenses and damage to Wilson's property that had been run up by Family members exceeded $100,000. Since no money was likely to be forthcoming from Manson, Wilson simply appropriated Manson's song "Cease to Exist" and reworked it into "Never Learn Not to Love," which appeared on the Beach Boys album *20/20*.

Wilson took the sole writing credit.

The recording artist may have seen his actions as justly getting a little back. But Manson, who had staked his ego on becoming a huge rock star, was incensed. On the one hand, it was another example of the Hollywood entertainment complex screwing him over. On the other, it was a major impediment on his rocket ride to fame and glory. His ego, his vanity, and his plans had taken big, simultaneous, hard-stop hits. Charlie Manson did not handle those kinds of blows well.

More than that, Wilson had changed the lyrics to the song. And just as Manson thought the songs on the *White Album* were carefully coded, so were the lyrics to "Cease to Exist." Manson's message had been destroyed.

Later, after the Tate/LaBianca murders, a shaken but grateful Wilson had this perspective: he would say he was one of the luckiest people to have come across the Family, because he only ended up losing money.

Despite their differences with Wilson, the relationship with Melcher was still ongoing—in Manson's eyes, at least. Tex Watson, whom Manson had met at Wilson's mansion, would end up joining Melcher at 10050 Cielo Drive around half a dozen times during the summer of 1968. And Watson was getting chummier with Manson.

By the fall of 1968, the Family was at the Spahn Ranch, but not exclusively. One of their hangouts was, during January and February of 1969, at 21019 Gresham Street in Canoga Park, a neighborhood in the San Fernando Valley. The house, which is no longer there, was a single-family home rented by Bill Vance, who had met Charlie in prison. Vance would occasionally let Family members crash there, and as Charlie's obsession with creating a record grew, Vance let the Family take the house over so they could set up a recording studio.

In keeping with Charlie's Beatles fascination, the private little retreat was nicknamed the "Yellow Submarine" in honor of its bright yellow exterior.

It was a four-bedroom home, and Charlie saw it as a better place than the desert to house his Family during the winter, although he did leave a handful of Family members—mostly girls—to keep on with the chores and make sure George Spahn did not forget about them.

Spahn Ranch, with its various distractions—chores Manson's Family had agreed to do—did not allow much time for members to practice their music. The Yellow Submarine did, and furthermore its four bedrooms would house a double handful of Family members comparatively comfortably.

Best of all, it had a large front room which, in Charlie's opinion, would serve perfectly as a recording studio. However, two employees at the Spahn Ranch were indirectly responsible for that plan never coming to fruition.

Donald "Shorty" Shea had worked at Spahn as an animal handler and general maintenance man since October 1962, well before the Family had shown up. Shea had been an on-again, off-again employee at the Spahn Ranch. He also was a manager at a strip club, ran adult bookstores in Las Vegas, and took mining and truck driving gigs when they came along.

All this was in addition to his low-level film career. Shea would do animal handling and stunt work during movie shoots, and even appeared onscreen in an uncredited role in a Prohibition-era gangster flick titled *The Fabulous Bastard from Chicago* (1969).

Shea's cousin, Windy Bucklee, was similarly employed-as-needed at Spahn Ranch. She had been a stagecoach driver in live Western shows.

Bucklee had been alarmed when the Manson Family moved in, as she saw them taking a family-friendly horse ranch and turning it into a hippie paradise, which meant minimum cleanliness and maximum nudity. She approved of neither.

Despite this, Bucklee kept to her side of the fence until Family business interfered with hers. In 1968, she was pulled over while driving her Ford truck. The police officer stopped her and explained her truck had been seen close by to where four small businesses had been robbed.

As she was able to prove she had clocked in at her job on the nights of the robberies, Bucklee was quickly removed from the suspect list. But she knew what had happened. Bill Vance, her neighbor, had a set of keys for the truck and would borrow it occasionally.

In a fury, Bucklee confronted Vance and demanded her keys back. A few hours later, Charlie Manson showed up at her home, demanding the keys. She told him to "fuck off," and he responded by hitting her face so hard it broke her jaw.

Bucklee somehow managed to get upstairs to her bedroom, where she kept a gun. Unfortunately, the gun she grabbed was a German Luger pistol someone had given to her, and she had not figured out its safety mechanism.

Had she known how to use it, Manson would have died right there.

Instead, he ran off.

Bucklee was in the hospital for three days, as her broken jaw needed to be wired shut. While Shea did not care how many people were in the Manson Family, he did have issue with Manson breaking Bucklee's jaw, and so ran over to Vance's house and confronted Charlie Manson, who had a knife and no qualms about fighting. Here, the messiah fell short. Shea beat the crap out of him and left him on the ground.

For Shea, the incident was over. But Manson had been beaten up in front of Family members. Instead of working that into a kind of revelation, a show of Christ-like humility, Manson seethed with vicious purpose. He would close up the Yellow Submarine house and move his operations back to Spahn Ranch, where the seemingly victorious Shea still worked. There, he would wait.

There is one more aspect to the Yellow Submarine house worth noting. According to Tate/LaBianca murder trial prosecutor Vincent Bugliosi, during the Family's brief stay both Paul Watkins and Brooks Poston heard Manson talk about slaughtering well-heeled "pigs" and writing things on walls with their blood.

Brooks Poston would be in a position to share these tidbits with investigators as a result of associating with Paul Crockett. Crockett, along with Melcher and Shea, were the three men who, at one point or another during 1969, would each impede Manson's path to glory.

At the beginning of 1969, Manson realized the Spahn Ranch was not going to be a sufficient stronghold when Helter Skelter came down. He had two other locations which were suitable: the Myers Ranch and the Barker Ranch, which was adjacent to Myers. The ranches were deep in mining country in Death Valley National Park, hours from Los Angeles, across rough roads and desert terrain.

Myers Ranch, for all its desolation, had amenities and buildings that made it livable. Barker Ranch offered much less in the way of comforts. There were no electric lines. It did, however, have water, thanks to a 5,000-gallon reservoir, and generators. Its buildings were strong—they were made of stone and concrete. It was perfect, as Manson explained to Arlene Barker, who owned the ranch, for musicians who wanted a quiet place to live while they made music, free from distractions. These included radio, as the ranch's remoteness meant it did not receive broadcasts well.

All this was fine for Manson. Where prospectors in the area once sought gold and uranium, all he wanted was some peace and quiet.

To seal the deal with Barker, Manson presented her with a gold Beach Boys record. Only a bona fide musician would have such a prize, right? Sources vary on whether Dennis Wilson had given the record to Manson or whether it had been unofficially "liberated" when the Family was forced out of his mansion. At any rate, it proved payment enough.

The isolation Manson sought offered protection from the race war he had convinced himself would happen. But there were also drawbacks. Few Family members were willing to brave the blasting heat of summer, the bitter cold of winter, the jerry-rigged utilities, and the incessant bugs. Anything that could not be grown near the ranch or taken from the land had to be trucked in. And the free-flowing drugs necessary to keep the Family obedient were largely supplied by ranch visitors. Spahn Ranch was much more accessible than Barker.

Nonetheless, Manson began sending Family members there with orders to determine how they could make it work.

Much like the act of killing, Manson did not want to do the dirty work himself. But in sending his small advance teams away from him, and not controlling their minds or drug intake, his control over them began to slip.

In March 1969, Paul Crockett, a lead prospector and site investigator for various mining companies, set up a small outpost near the two ranches. His partner, Bob Berry, had been in the area for several months, scouting for mining sites— but also enjoying the hospitality offered by the Manson girls who occasionally stayed at Barker. One in particular, Juanita Wildebush, had captured his fancy.

Crockett was less impressed. Wildebush and another Family member, Brooks Poston, had described the Family dynamics to him, and Crockett was disturbed by Manson's control over the followers. The kids the forty-five-year-old miner was meeting seemed zombified, which was bad enough. Depending on whom he was speaking with, as Family members came in and out of Barker, he got a picture of a little man with a huge messiah complex. Watkins had a grounding in Scientology and mysticism, and realized how much Manson was twisting these.

Furthermore, the apocalyptic ramblings about Helter Skelter that came out in bits and pieces ranged from fantastic to incoherent. But as Crockett spent evenings speaking with Manson Family kids, he saw something else: fear.

Even though Manson was more than 200 miles away, those at the Barker Ranch felt closely tied to him. If they had any doubts or impulses to leave, they were deeply buried.

The more Crockett heard about Manson, the more he saw the skinny, nervous kids who were coming in and out of Barker, and felt the need to step in. His first steps in deprogramming Family members were strikingly similar to what Manson had used to entrap them. Crockett persuaded a few of them to join him in prospecting work. The work was physically demanding, involving digging, shoveling, lifting, and hauling rocks, and Crockett was not shy about pushing the kids to their limits. It was a far cry from the easier life at Spahn Ranch, but the kids who did it found themselves getting physically stronger as their minds cleared.

Even so, not every Family member who came to the Barker Ranch was enticed by Crockett. Some, when they returned to Manson at the Spahn Ranch, reported that a paternal figure had been getting close to some of his Family. At some point, Manson was going to have to intervene.

Instead, in May 1969, he sent Paul Watkins to investigate. Unfortunately for Manson, there was one more conversion tactic Crockett borrowed from him. Both Watkins and Poston had an interest in music. Crockett didn't share this enthusiasm, but found a way around it.

"Every person has his own music, the things he listens to, the things that harmonize in his universe," Crockett later said. "So I thought, I don't need to teach [them] anything about music if I can get *him* [meaning Manson] out" of their heads.

Just as had been the case with Poston, Watkins found Crockett's folksy mysticism—in truth, opportunism and counter-Scientology programming—attractive. If Manson had realized the depth of Crockett's influence, he likely would not have let Watkins stay at Barker Ranch through mid-August. But Watkins was surprisingly good at keeping one foot in each camp. Under Crockett's urging, Poston and Watkins would start a band, calling themselves Desert Sun. It did not go anywhere commercially, but it had a much bigger impact metaphysically. In essence, it would eventually be part of what freed them.

Juanita Wildebush would find freedom in a different way. She and Bob Berry, Crockett's mining partner, would run off and get married.

Manson and Crockett would maintain an uneasy peace throughout the summer; this was mostly because Manson was focused on his recording career. It was sure to take off at any moment, he thought, and so he needed to stay close to Los Angeles.

In addition, July and August would yield other, more pressing concerns. Tragically for many people, the start of a brilliant music career for Charlie Manson was not one of them.

Terry Melcher had not had any contact with Manson since the Family had been thrown out of Wilson's mansion the summer before. Nonetheless, in mid-March 1969, Manson got it into his head that Melcher was coming to the Spahn Ranch to audition his music—and even imagined a specific day!

Manson and the Family launched into a frenzy of cleaning, baking, joint-rolling, and choreographing. On the day of Melcher's arrival, there would be a focus on Manson, with a choir of his girls singing backup. Both Manson and Melcher would be positioned so that nature would also play a part in the performance. It was not going to be an audition; it was going to be an experience.

Melcher never showed up and, once again, Manson was humiliated in front of his Family.

But he was not one to give up so easily. He had never forgotten being in the car when Dennis Wilson dropped Melcher at his home. And so, on May 23, without any advance notice, Manson arrived at 10050 Cielo Drive.

Manson initially walked around the front yard, perhaps composing how he would approach Melcher. He was spotted by someone inside—Iranian photojournalist Shahrokh Hatami, who had been visiting the home's current resident.

Hatami went out on the front porch of the home and confronted the stranger. He did not know the name Melcher, but thought the stranger might be a friend of the man who actually owned the property—Rudi Altobelli, whom Manson had met earlier at Dennis Wilson's mansion. Altobelli, as it happened, was staying in one of the houses behind the main house.

Altobelli being on premises was a rarity. He usually did not stay at the estate, preferring to make it available for entertainment luminaries such as actors Samantha Eggar, Henry Fonda, and Olivia Hussey—all former tenants. Cary Grant and Dyan Cannon had even used it as their honeymoon retreat four years earlier.

Had Manson known more about the person who had spoken with him, he might not have been so quick to scurry away. Hatami had photographed The Beatles during their early days, when they were performing in Liverpool's Cavern Club. If nothing else, Manson would have taken their interaction as a further sign of his destiny.

But then one of the current residents, having heard the conversation, came to the door. And for a very brief moment, Charlie Manson and Sharon Tate stared at each other. Without saying hello, or anything else, Manson left.

Manson returned to the guest house later in the day. He found Altobelli packing, as he and Tate were leaving for Rome the next morning. Manson introduced himself, but Altobelli was dismissive, pointing out they had met the previous summer.

Manson started by asking where Melcher was, and Altobelli lied, saying he did not know. He did—Melcher and Bergen had moved to Malibu—but Altobelli was not going to tell Manson that.

Manson tried several times to engage Altobelli, but Altobelli dismissed him.

Through one means or another Melcher did eventually promise to come out to the Spahn Ranch in May and listen to Manson perform. Melcher never addressed what had happened in March—whether he was scheduled to come to the ranch and forgot, or whether he never knew about the supposed audition.

Once again, Manson threw the Family into a frenzy of cleaning and rehearsal.

Melcher showed up with Gregg Jakobson, an acquaintance of Tex Watson who was also in the industry. The two were all business; Melcher was there to listen to Manson's music, not to partake in any of the Family's other offerings. He did not want to talk to Manson about world philosophies or anything else. Nor did he want sex with any of the Manson girls.

Melcher heard Manson play for about an hour. Manson was the lead singer, of course, but from time to time a choir of Family members would join in. Some banged on tambourines while others clapped.

When the concert was over, Melcher asked Manson a few questions, mostly practical—such as if he was in any musicians' unions, such as the AFL or AFTRA. He was not, he said. But inside he had to be thinking, *of course not*. Messiahs do not need to belong to unions.

But people who wanted to be recorded in a professional studio did. Without union membership there would be no serious recording effort—despite what Dennis Wilson had done earlier for Manson.

With the conversation unhelpfully concluded, Melcher sought a way to excuse himself. As a courtesy, and because many of the Family members looked hungry and were clearly living in the squalor of the Spahn Ranch, Melcher handed Manson fifty dollars and left. He had made no indication of commitment about the music one way or another.

To Manson, that was little different from an outright rejection. He was again faced with a potential humiliation in front of his Family. There was no big recording contract signing. Nobody fell and kissed the singer's feet. There was no promise of a major record release, which would have funded preparations in advance of Helter Skelter. And absent that money, Manson was going to have a difficult time keeping his Family safe.

Angry and disappointed and unable to keep one from fueling the other, Manson fell back on his usual strategy of saying or doing whatever it would take to keep their confidence for however long he could. As long as he kept telling people what they wanted to hear, he would be able to stay afloat.

Giving Manson the money was a kind mistake, but Melcher would soon make another one. Privately, he told Jakobson that he was not interested in recording Manson, but that he would be willing to bring a friend, Mike Deasy, who had a mobile recording unit he used to tape Hopi Indian music, to the ranch. There was no way Manson was going to be able to set foot in a studio without union membership.

In June, Melcher arranged for Deasy to join him and Jakobson at the Spahn Ranch. The excursion lasted for three days, and was a disaster. Deasy got hold of some bad acid, and his resulting trip was a nightmare. There is no record, one way or another, of anything being recorded on the four-track unit in Deasy's trailer.

On the third day, Deasy was still in bad shape and needed to leave. Jakobson, Manson, and Melcher were bringing him back to a car that would take him home, when they were approached by forty-seven-year-old Randy Starr. In addition to being an occasional ranch hand, Starr was also the husband of Windy Bucklee, the woman whose jaw Manson had broken.

Starr was obviously, almost comically, drunk. He was also in a fighting mood, waving a gun around though not really pointing it at anyone. Fortunately, he was not in a condition to fight. Unfortunately for him, Manson, who had seen the promise of recording time go down the outhouse hole during the prior three days, was.

Manson let his anger out and began viciously beating Starr. Deasy, Jakobson, and Melcher got in their car as fast as they could and left.

A few days later, Melcher called Manson and tried to give him the ego-preserving brush off he used with other acts. The talent was there, Melcher would say, but as a producer he was not sure how he could shape it. Best of luck, take care.

Goodbye, recording career. Goodbye, funding for Helter Skelter preparations.

Like the petty crimes of his past—the simple check scam that involved going into a mailbox, making it a federal crime, the pimping rap that he compounded by taking girls across state lines, a likely probation sentence that he turned into jail time by jumping bail—over the next two months, Charlie Manson was going to make a series of bad decisions.

This time, however, the consequences would shake the entire country.

CHAPTER FIVE

"You assume what you would do in my position, but that doesn't mean that is what I did in my position. It doesn't mean that my philosophy is valid. It's only valid to me. Your philosophies, they are whatever you think they are and I don't particularly care what you think they are."
—CHARLES MANSON, COURT STATEMENT, NOVEMBER 19, 1970

Charlie Manson did not fear the law. He did not fear the courts. He did not fear societal rejection. He did not even fear his Family's rejection, as so far he had been able to bluff his way out through any seeming setbacks.

After all, those were all things that Jesus had faced . . . and conquered.

But Manson's time in jail did teach him to fear black militants. And by the time he was released in 1967, the Black Panther movement, launched in 1966, was openly calling for rebellion in the streets.

Manson did not want to hear or see that, nor did he want to upset or distract the Family. As such, he restricted media coming into the various Family strongholds. While most Family members had, at best, a cursory knowledge of current events, Manson was free to consume what he wanted during his offsite trips. It was likely that the rage boiling through urban pockets put added fire in his own belly. He had to be prepared. Surrounded by a fundamentally ignorant Family, and with no one to provide countering viewpoints to news stories, he had an echo chamber to amplify his views.

One of his views was that the Black Panthers, those he had seen taking power in prisons and on the streets, were coming for the white man.

The result was a heightened desire in Manson to move the Family from Spahn Ranch deeper into the desert, where it could be armed and fortified.

But moving the Family's operations and stocking up on fuel, food, and ammunition was expensive. While the Family had gotten along on petty crime and milking sympathizers for whatever they (or their parents) could provide, Manson needed a sizable cash infusion, and fast.

Dumpster diving, panhandling, drug deals, car thefts, and various petty crimes such as credit card fraud, along with claiming the possessions of those joining the Family, had more or less met the Family's financial needs through the early part of 1969. But recruitment had waned, and the streets of San Francisco and Los Angeles had been overrun with hippies seeking handouts.

Even a half-formed plan to have the prettier of the Manson girls sign up with strip clubs came to no avail: the waiflike beauties Manson attracted, with the exception of Susan Atkins, who had been a topless dancer, were unemployably small-chested. Even applying all their skills, the ladies would never have passed an audition; prostitution obviously ran risks with the law.

Charles "Tex" Watson hatched a get-cash-quick scheme with Manson. Like so many of Manson's other criminal capers, it was poorly thought out and poorly executed. The plan's one saving grace was that, since it involved ripping off a drug dealer, chances were good the authorities would not get involved.

Watson contacted Luella, one of his ex-girlfriends who herself was a low-level drug dealer. Luella was to contact a mid-level drug dealer named Bernard "Lotsapoppa" Crowe and offer him 25 kilos of marijuana for $2,500.

Lotsapoppa might have trusted Luella, but he definitely did not trust the scruffy white man who appeared in front of him on July 1, 1969. Rather than just turn the cash over, he decided to drive Luella and Tex to the supposed rendezvous site. As an extra precaution, Luella was to stay in Lotsapoppa's Cadillac while Watson fetched the drugs.

Lotsapoppa's plan would have worked if Watson had still possessed even a drop of affection for Luella . . . but he did not. Watson went in the front of the apartment building where his connections supposedly lived and out the back. He met up with Family member Thomas "TJ" Walleman and the two headed back to Spahn Ranch, with the cash but without Luella.

Charlie Manson was now $2,500 richer, but had a new and substantial problem. Lotsapoppa took Luella back to her apartment and immediately called Spahn Ranch, demanding to speak to "Charles" and, more importantly, the return of his money. Manson took the call and claimed Watson had split the ranch weeks earlier; he had no idea where he was. Lotsapoppa did not believe him, and said he would come to the ranch either to collect or kill every Family member he could find. Manson might have a double handful of hippie children, Lotsapoppa said, but the black man? He had access to a posse of armed Black Panthers.

That last part was a lie. Lotsapoppa was not a Black Panther, nor did he have any pull to round up such a crew. The lie, however, played right into Manson's paranoia. Manson contacted Lotsapoppa and arranged a meeting, ostensibly to discuss the matter. But like the drug deal itself, there was little truth to this.

Manson corralled TJ Walleman into joining him. Walleman was a twenty-six-year-old former Marine who had been living at the Spahn ranch for a few years and had embraced the mysticism of the demented guru. While Walleman left the ranch before the Tate/LaBianca killings, he would return once Manson was in prison. As he would tell *Rolling Stone* magazine, the attitude among Family members was "I am Charlie. When he dies, I die. I gave up my personality and became what he showed me I could be."

That did not prove to be the case with Walleman. He was not a murderer, despite his military background. When Manson tapped him, the original plan had been for the two to meet "Lotsapoppa" Crowe at Luella's apartment. Both men would be armed. Upon a pre-arranged signal, Walleman was to kill Lotsapoppa; Manson would not draw his weapon. Manson would later claim he had "cut up some people and shot some people" but always denied killing anyone. As per his usual modus operandi, he was going to let someone else do the dirty work.

Manson and Walleman arrived at Luella's apartment. Lotsapoppa was flanked by a couple of his business associates. The conversation spun out of control within minutes, quickly reaching the point where Walleman *should* have taken action, once again keeping Manson from actually committing murder. But, instead, Walleman froze.

Manson did not. Rage and impatience overcoming reason, fear of punishment, or any other inhibition, Manson drew a .22 caliber Buntline revolver and pulled the trigger three times. The gun offered up a sickly *click, click, click*; the first three pulls were misfires. With the fourth, as the bigger man lunged at him to seize the weapon, it produced a modest report and Lotsapoppa was shot in the stomach.

The bullet stopped a fraction of an inch from the big man's spine, yet Lotsapoppa fell to the floor. He was not dead, and would not die from the wound, but Manson assumed he was; which, in Manson's thinking, meant he had killed a Black Panther drug lord. And that would mean heavy repercussions. If word spread among the black community, Manson's plan for Helter Skelter would start sooner than he could prepare. Furthermore, his potential post–racial war role as a leader of black society would be seriously compromised.

Walleman had a more immediate concern. He had seen Manson's occasional rages and knew he was a marked man. And so he fled, although he would reappear during the trial as a key prosecution witness, asserting that Manson himself was capable of murder, not just manipulating others to do it.

Another huge shock for Manson would come later when the dead man himself, Bernard "Lotsapoppa" Crowe, appeared on the stand to testify against him.

Manson's misconception about Crowe's death was furthered by an unrelated incident. Right around the time of the Crowe shooting, there were rumors of the body of a Black Panther found on one of the campuses of UCLA. The rumors were sketchy, and they may have originated with widely reported accounts of two Black Panthers having been shot to death on a UCLA campus in January 1969. But news filtered to the Spahn Ranch in dribbles, and it would have been easy for Manson and the other Family members to scramble the stories.

The war, it appeared, was about to start.

Time was now Manson's latest foe. The timetable for the Helter Skelter vision he had outlined during the New Year's Eve bonfire had to be sped up. That meant arming the Family, and that meant more money—the exact predicament that had led him to shoot Crowe.

Manson would not have flat-out expressed his financial concerns, but he was enough of a manipulator to let them be known. His Family members, perpetually eager to please him, would have been primed to come up with a story that would make him happy, even if it were not true. Live in the moment, as Charlie said.

Susan Atkins and Ella Jo Bailey had been roommates before joining the Family.

While traveling with Manson, one or both would have likely crashed at the home of Gary Hinman, a doctoral student who was studying sociology at UCLA.

Hinman, a practicing Buddhist, was known within the counterculture for being a soft touch for a place to stay; his home in Topanga Canyon was open to all who needed it.

Unlike many in the counterculture, Hinman was not struggling to get by. He owned his home, had a couple of vehicles, and in addition to his studies had regular gigs as a music teacher. To kids who had been trained to scour through garbage bins for food, it would seem as though he had a fortune.

When the Family's money problems began to surface, Atkins and Bailey may well have started speculating on how large that fortune really was. With each retelling of what Hinman had done for people, or what they had seen in his home, his holdings doubtlessly grew. He had stocks and bonds. He had an inheritance. He was worth $20,000. The details were sketchy, but that one number—even if Atkins and Bailey had come up with it themselves—was intriguing.

There were other rumors, too. Hinman also had a degree in chemistry, and according to some sources was not above brewing a little mescaline in a basement lab.

Bobby Beausoleil was one of the more strident advocates of this theory. He would eventually present it during his murder trial—for the killing of Gary Hinman.

Beausoleil held he had resold some mescaline he had gotten from Hinman to the Straight Satans motorcycle gang. Unfortunately, the drugs were either tainted with strychnine or ineffective, according to whoever was telling the story. At any rate, the Straight Satans were understandably not pleased and wanted their money back. Manson was not pleased, either; the money from the drug sale was supposed to help support the Family.

On July 25, 1969, at Manson's urging, Beausoleil, Atkins, and Mary Brunner went to Hinman's home. Atkins and Brunner went in first, hoping that the two girls would lull Hinman into a false sense of security. The arrangement was that if Hinman was alone, one would stand at a window and signal for Beausoleil to join them.

Hinman was alone, but he was not interested in joining the Family. As for money, he either refused to give it to them or just did not have it. He probably did not. Despite Beausoleil brutally assaulting Hinman, no money was forthcoming.

Frustrated, Beausoleil called Manson at the Spahn Ranch and told him Hinman was being uncooperative. What should he do?

Charlie decided to answer in person. He drove the 20 miles from Spahn Ranch to Hinman's home with Bruce Davis in tow. Frustrated with his underling, Manson was eager to assert his personal strength and supremacy . . . and to teach. Teaching was important. Hinman answered the door, bloodied and patched up, but still capable of walking and talking.

Manson entered Hinman's home swinging a cutlass he had taken from Danny DeCarlo, cutting deep gashes in Hinman's face. "I showed Bobby [Beausoleil] how to stand up like a man," Manson would later say. "He had a woman's thoughts."

Message delivered to both Beausoleil and Hinman. Manson and Davis left the house, with the latter taking one of Hinman's cars.

Atkins, Beausoleil, and Brunner parked themselves in Hinman's home for two days, standing watch over him, discussing his fate, and emptying his fridge and cupboards. Beausoleil also beat Hinman with the butt of a gun. During one of the heavier blows the gun went off, sending a stray bullet underneath the kitchen sink.

Hinman underwent two days of home "care" by Atkins and Brunner, which included stitching up his ear with dental floss, as well as additional threats. During their time there, Atkins answered Hinman's phone when it rang. She would put on an English accent and tell the caller Hinman had gone to Colorado, as his parents had been in an automobile accident.

Hinman finally signed over the registrations to his two vehicles, but at one point, he said the magic words "I'm going to go to the police."

Would he have? Or was it just a desperate plea? It's hard to say—but it may have been enough to convince the Family he had to die.

Beausoleil mentioned the police to Charlie during a phone call on Sunday, July 27. Charlie's response was that Beausoleil "knew what to do"—without actually spelling out what the next step was. Beausoleil understood.

Despite what he thought had happened with Bernard Crowe, there was no way

Manson was going to be around for another killing. Perhaps this was a lesson from prison: if killing is inevitable, plant the seed and leave without doing or even seeing anything.

On July 27, the three Family members staying with Hinman ended the charade. Beausoleil stabbed Hinman twice, and all three took turns holding a pillow over his face as he bled out. The three sought to throw suspicion to . . . pretty much anyone. Someone recalled Manson's rants about the uprising of militant blacks. To spur Helter Skelter, or so the theory went, Beausoleil emphatically printed POLITICAL PIGGY on a wall in Hinman's blood. Just to make absolutely sure the blame would be placed where it was supposed to go, Beausoleil used a little more blood to print an animal paw on the wall, immediately to the left of the word PIGGY.

Hinman's body was not discovered until four days later, when concerned friends went to his home, smelled something dead—a distinct and not unfamiliar odor in Southern California—and saw flies buzzing around one of the windows of the house. Police were called, and detectives found Hinman's mangled body, face-up on its back. Hinman had been left to rot on his living room floor. A tangle of Buddhist prayer beads were found close to his body. Detectives also discovered the 9-millimeter bullet which had lodged under the sink.

Perhaps inevitably, and certainly ironically, in the investigation that followed, no evidence of a large inheritance ever surfaced.

For the first time, the Family had taken a life. Beausoleil was so pleased with himself that he boasted to Danny DeCarlo, the resident Straight Satans motorcycle club member, about what he had done. If Hinman had sold bad mescaline and Beausoleil had given it to the Straight Satans, surely the motorcycle club's treasurer would want to know the account had been balanced.

Beausoleil also showed off one of the weapons he had used. It was a Mexican Bowie knife that had designs etched on the blade and a distinctive metal animal head on the shaft. Beausoleil loved the knife, and despite DeCarlo's urging he discard it because it had been used in a murder, he refused to do so.

The knife was not the only evidence from Hinman's murder the Family had brought back to the ranch. The Family had driven Hinman's two vehicles—a white Fiat station wagon and a Volkswagen microbus—to Spahn Ranch. Ella Jo

Bailey would later testify that while cleaning it she noticed there was no key to the microbus; it had been hotwired.

Even though the Family had ownership slips signed over to them, there was bound to be lots of uncomfortable questions around the wagon and microbus, which had been reported missing. Strip them, sell them, leave them somewhere far away from the Family—any of these would have been obvious, if not smart, actions.

What was *not* smart was driving one of the cars, the station wagon, until it broke down on a stretch of U.S. Route 101 near San Luis Obispo, California. Yet that is exactly what Beausoleil did on August 6, 1969. According to DeCarlo, Manson told Beausoleil to take the car down to the valley, wipe it clean, and dump it. Either feeling invincible, a little shell-shocked, or just plain stupid—possibly all three—Beausoleil did not.

Police saw the car sitting on the shoulder just before 11 a.m. Beausoleil, who had been sleeping in the back, presented the officers with the owner's certificate and the registration papers, but claimed he did not have any other identification, such as a driver's license.

Ever mindful of Manson's Helter Skelter delusions, Beausoleil claimed that he had purchased the station wagon from a black man a week prior. His driver's license and other identification were in a pickup truck he had been driving.

Beausoleil said he had paid $200 cash for it, which, he offered, might account for some of the confusion. What definitely added to the confusion was the false name and birthdate he gave.

Within minutes, dispatchers confirmed what the police suspected: the car had been stolen. Beausoleil was immediately arrested for auto theft.

At the police station, officers made another discovery. The stolen vehicle report was not signed by the previous owner because the previous owner—Gary Hinman—was dead. By the time Beausoleil's wallet yielded a credit card in the name of Sheryl A. McAdams, there was no more confusion. Bobby Beausoleil was hit with a new charge, this time for murder.

There was a third discovery, which was the most damning. In one of the tire wells of the station wagon, police found Beausoleil's prized Mexican Bowie knife.

Beausoleil's arrest was going to bring unwanted attention to the Family at

Spahn Ranch, yet Manson was not ready to move the Family deeper into the desert in order to avoid Helter Skelter. The Barker Ranch in Death Valley still needed work. Beausoleil had to be quickly and decisively cleared of involvement in the Hinman killing.

The Family came up with a plan, of sorts—a sick double-or-quit solution in which the decision was to double down. If the killers who had left a paw print on Gary Hinman's wall would kill again, leaving similar marks, it would vindicate Beausoleil, or so the acid-inspired logic around Spahn Ranch held. The only necessary element was a target important enough that it would get media attention, and a setting at least moderately familiar to Manson so that he could seemingly come up with an inspired plan.

While Manson may not have shared this with too many other people, there was at least one individual who fit that bill—the people now in the former home of the big-shot record producer who had humiliated him in front of his Family, the one whose home Manson knew was isolated: Terry Melcher.

There was an additional benefit, or so it seemed. By guiding his followers to pull off a successful murder, Manson would again show he was in control. Manson, master criminal, had inside information about the estate, and the goal was to avoid any more of his people getting caught.

There was just one stumbling block. Rudi Altobelli had already told Manson Melcher was no longer living at 10050 Cielo Drive. Manson confirmed that when he had gone by Melcher's new residence in Malibu, stealing a telescope. He intended it as a warning message to show he could always find him. Nonetheless, 10050 Cielo Drive was accessible and remote. It was still an ideal spot, assuming there were an ideal resident. And it was a plan with an added benefit: throwing a good scare into Melcher, the former resident, would be payback for the musician he had so openly and condescendingly spurned.

Manson did not tell his Family any of this. He knew who lived at the house. He had been there alone in March 1969 looking for Melcher. Shahrokh Hatami said Sharon Tate had come to the door that day and Manson had seen her. He also confirmed he told Charles the Polanskis lived at the residence.

But had Manson had more contact with Tate before? How well did he really know the glamorous up-and-coming movie star and did he have more of a reason to exact some revenge? She was said to have been to the Spahn Ranch and enjoyed riding the horses. Some of her band of "turned-on" pals had been scoring drugs from somewhere, and Charles "Tex" Watson was a well-known supplier. Did he know Tate or Sebring? Or perhaps Wojciech Frykowski? Had Watson or Manson ever come face to face with Roman Polanski himself? It was certainly possible; the Manson Family had been making money selling drugs and were already infamous on the Hollywood party scene. Altobelli himself would later testify he had met Manson before, saying they were at a party together and listened to a recording of Manson's songs.

Manson's confidante Marlin Marynick claims they did, saying: "There are things that are not really common knowledge, because people only want to see the manic cult leader. Charlie was a functioning musician; Neil Young gave him a motorbike and he hung out with Jim Morrison, and Mama Cass was a friend of his. She was supposed to speak at his trial. That's the circles they moved in, everybody knew each other in Hollywood.

"When I asked him about Sharon Tate he said they were his friends and he knew them . . . he went swimming there. They all knew each other; it wasn't a random thing and I think when you go into it, it's all over drugs."

That theory is shared by Jim Markham, the protégé of Jay Sebring who took over his businesses after the murders and went on to become a haircare multi-millionaire.

Sebring had long been rumored to have dealt drugs to the stars whose hair he cut from his salons. While Markham didn't want to elaborate on that detail, he told The Hollywood Reporter in 2019: "I believe Manson had gone up to the house and wanted to sell cocaine and marijuana.

"He showed Jay and Wojciech the product. They were going to buy some of it, but the two of them beat him up at the gate.

"The next night, Manson sent the Family up [to kill them].

"I've lived with that for 50 years. I still believe that."

The drug deal theory was popular after the murders and before Manson and his gang were caught, but fell out of history once prosecutor Vincent Bugliosi started to focus the motive for the killings on the Helter Skelter race war.

For his part Manson—always conscious of his public image and, through time, a proven unreliable narrator—would never admit to any reason for the killings, maintaining publicly the attack was random.

In a 1976 interview with the *National Enquirer*, he said: "It didn't matter who was killed as long as it was someone.

"No one picked out Sharon Tate and went down there and plotted a course for madness. You have to understand the episode.

"It was a soul movement—children willing to rise up and change the world. How else were we going to wake up the people that don't know we cannot destroy our children's world?

"I wasn't there in the house that night, but I was there in spirit."

There were other factors as well. Manson was a jealous man whose career was stalling, and so needed a lift and to cause a splash. What would have more impact than killing an eight-month-pregnant Hollywood actress?

He had already gotten his followers to kill for him once. Why not do it again and choose a bigger target, such as some rich and glamorous piggies?

Manson would ensure the beautiful young actress who had everything, her spoiled pals, and her rich, successful husband knew the party was over. Manson, the perpetual outsider looking in at Hollywood glory, would have his revenge on those who had shunted him aside.

* * *

The tragic death of his wife and unborn baby was the latest in a series of incredibly sad episodes to befall thirty-five-year-old Polish film director Roman Polanski.

He had been born in Paris in 1933, but his parents moved the family to Poland in 1937, and were subsequently forced by the Nazis to live in the Jewish ghetto in Krakow, Poland. His mother later died at the Auschwitz death camp but Polanski and his father, who had been sent to a work camp, were reunited after World War II.

Polanski survived the Holocaust by living with a series of foster parents who raised him to act as a Roman Catholic; he would later declare himself an atheist.

Polanski then attended the National Film School in Lodz, Poland, where he wrote and directed several short films.

Polanski burst onto the professional cinema scene with his first full-length feature, the sexual-tension drama *Knife in the Water* (1962), which he co-wrote and directed. He then followed his much-lauded debut with the powerful psycho-sexual drama *Repulsion* (1965). In 1968 he would find commercial success with his adaptation of Ira Levin's novel *Rosemary's Baby,* which opened the gateway to Hollywood for him, but it was his previous film, the 1967 comedic horror *The Fearless Vampire Killers, or Pardon Me, But Your Teeth Are in My Neck*—known in Europe as *Dance of the Vampires*—which featured a twenty-three-year-old actress whose beauty dominated every scene she was in, and whom he would marry. Her name was Sharon Tate.

Acting was a curious career choice for Tate. Her father had been an Army officer, and when Tate was a child her family moved frequently. She made few solid friendships, and her shyness underscored her social discomfort.

Tate was pretty and her first recognition came on the runway, from an early age, as she was entered into beauty pageants. By the time she graduated high school in 1961 she had also done extra work and appeared in small film and television roles.

By 1963, Tate had moved to Los Angeles, and eased into acting with small roles in television productions including the shows *Mr. Ed* and *The Beverly Hillbillies.*

She overcame her shyness enough to date during her early Hollywood years and in 1964 met Jay Sebring, a high-end men's hair stylist. Sebring's gentle nature played well with Tate's shyness, and the two became very close.

Sebring eventually proposed marriage, but she turned him down.

In 1966, Tate finally landed a major film role in the gothic horror *Eye of the Devil* (1967). Her performance convinced her manager she was ready for larger roles, and he booked her for what would be her most lauded role in *Valley of the Dolls* and also convinced Polanski to cast her as the lead in *Dance of the Vampires.*

Neither Polanski nor Tate were impressed with each other when they first met in London. Tate was talented but inexperienced, and Polanski demanded perfection from his actors. During filming, however, the two worked well together and Polanski was so taken with Tate's on-screen presence he wanted to cast her in *Rosemary's Baby,* but she lost out to Mia Farrow.

By the time production wrapped on *Dance of the Vampires,* Polanski and Tate had started a relationship, which shocked Sebring.

Like Polanski, Sebring was nine years older than Tate. Additionally, both had been on the rise. Sebring—born Thomas John Kummer—was making his mark in Los Angeles as a hair stylist with a client list including Doors lead singer Jim Morrison, actors Warren Beatty and Steve McQueen, and crooner Frank Sinatra. A Sebring haircut cost twenty-five times the going rate of a barbershop trim.

By the time Sebring met Tate, he had begun capitalizing on his business acumen. He had started training Markham and franchised his salons, opening on both coasts in the United States and in England.

Sebring indulged in the playboy lifestyle, jetting around to his business operations and hobnobbing with Hollywood luminaries. But losing Sharon Tate shook him. Despite this he and Polanski became friends, and Sebring was able, albeit reluctantly, to transition from a romantic relationship to a very close friendship with Tate.

Polanski had very specific ideas about what his married life would be like. He was not inclined toward monogamy, and wanted the couple to embrace his vision of the hippie lifestyle, which was freewheeling, inclusive, with an eye toward a perpetual party.

As part of this attitude, the couple, who rented a series of homes throughout 1968 and early 1969, had an open-door policy that encouraged friends and strangers alike to stop in whenever they were so inclined, alcohol and drugs were handed out freely and hippie ideas embraced.

Not only that, one biographer, Ed Sanders, claimed in his book *Sharon Tate: A Life* that Polanski would hold sex parties at the home and he'd film himself, his wife and their friends in decadent orgies, which he would later watch back with his pals.

Hatami claimed to Sanders that Polanski was also very controlling of his reluctant wife and "imposed" other girls and sexual fantasies onto her for his "sadomasochistic-porno movies"—which also featured a number of recognizable Hollywood faces.

No evidence of these videos actually existing has ever been presented.

For all his partying lifestyle, Sebring had few close friends, and was desperate to keep contact with Tate and the crowd she and Polanski moved in. In 1968, Polanski and Tate sought to expand his circle by introducing one of Polanski's childhood friends, aspiring screenwriter Wojciech Frykowski. Frykowski's ambitions were greater than his talent, as Polanski would later admit; but they were old pals.

Frykowski, in turn, introduced into the group his girlfriend Abigail Folger, a society maid and great-granddaughter of J.A. Folger, founder of the Folgers Coffee Company. Abigail Folger would soon invest in Sebring's operations, allowing him to expand his franchise empire.

Tate and Polanski continued working. In 1969, she took a comedic role in *Twelve Plus One* (1969) co-starring Orson Welles and Terry Thomas. The filming, which was done in early 1969, would take her throughout Europe. Her pregnancy, then in its second trimester, was covered by artful accessories such as handbags and scarves.

It would be Tate's last film role. She would not live to see it released.

Polanski, meanwhile, had been tapped to direct *The Day of the Dolphin* (1973). By spring 1969, both would leave for Europe to work on their films.

Before leaving, Tate and Polanski rented the home at 10050 Cielo Drive from Rudi Altobelli. The main house was a ranch-style structure with three bedrooms and four bathrooms. It offered more than enough room for the couple and their baby, which was due in late August. Some of the rooms had painted wood beams or stone walls. The estate featured a swimming pool and a guest house, where a caretaker lived. It was surrounded, and to some extent shielded, by pine and cherry trees.

Tate called it her "love house."

Tate and Polanski were familiar with the home before they moved in, as they had been inside it in 1968, when visiting its previous tenants, their friends Terry Melcher, Candice Bergen, and Roger Hart. The estate had become available when Melcher and Bergen had split up.

Polanski and Tate signed a one-year lease in February 1969, shortly after Melcher and Bergen moved out.

Tate had traveled after wrapping filming on *Twelve Plus One*, but by midsummer she wanted to be back in Los Angeles. She was close to giving birth, and wanted to have her child in the United States. In late July, she made the transatlantic voyage on the *Queen Elizabeth 2*. She was alone on that trip, Polanski had promised he would be home by August 12, in time for their child's due date.

At the time of his wife's murder, Polanski had been scouting locations for *The Day of the Dolphin* in London. Upon receiving the horrific news, Polanski immediately left the production.

* * *

If the lives and careers of Folger, Frykowski, Sebring, and Tate were in the process of flowering, Leno and Rosemary LaBianca were planning for their autumn harvest, a time when they would live in comfortable semi-retirement.

During the summer of 1969, the LaBiancas were trying desperately to get rid of their Spanish-style house at 3301 Waverly Drive. It had been where Leno had lived on and off since high school.

Leno had been a smart high school student and, by 1942, had started college and working at his father's wholesale and retail grocery businesses. In November 1943, he was drafted and joined the US effort in World War II. He married his first wife, Alice, shortly before leaving.

Upon returning in 1946, he settled into the Waverly Drive house with Alice where they had three children, and Leno took over the family grocery business in 1951. He and Alice split four years later and, growing tired of the grocery business, he harbored dreams of becoming a race horse breeder.

In 1959, Leno met thirty-seven-year-old Rosemary Struthers, a Mexican-born divorced mother of two. Like Leon's first wife, Rosemary was pretty and had a head for business. Later that year, they married in Las Vegas.

The couple flourished. Leno was already a successful grocer, and Rosemary's clothing shop, Boutique Carriage, was successful. By 1962, they had purchased a 6,000-square-foot home Walt Disney had commissioned in 1932. The structure was grand, but too much for the LaBiancas, especially as their children had left the nest. By 1968, the cost of maintaining it had outstripped their enjoyment. Leno sold it and used the proceeds to buy the Waverly Drive house from his mother.

Leno's return to Waverly Drive was supposed to be temporary. In early 1969, he negotiated a buyout deal with the shareholders of his grocery business that would have left him wealthy enough to build a horse ranch far from Los Angeles.

Leno and Rosemary may or may not have known Harold True, their former next-door neighbor, but Charlie Manson had become pals with him in prison. True had even given a ride to Manson on the day Manson left Terminal Island in 1967, and the two had stayed in touch. When Manson and his Family were making their rounds of the Los Angeles music scene, they would go to the occasional party at the home True shared with a few fellow UCLA students.

Manson was familiar with the LaBianca house, which he would later claim during one of his visits to True. At one point he had slipped out and into the LaBianca home when nobody was there, seeking a quiet place to rest or have sex. Entering was easy enough. In the years before the Manson Family killings, doors in the area often had minimal locks or were left open.

A year or so later, Manson would recall the house as a good location for a murder when he needed one.

In contrast to the comforts of the Tate and LaBianca homesteads, the Manson Family's hold on its digs at the Spahn Ranch were getting a lot more tenuous.

By August 1969, George Spahn had agreed to sell a substantial chunk of his ranch to a neighbor, Frank Retz. There was just one condition: Retz wanted the Manson Family gone. Spahn suggested that Retz hire ranch hand Donald Shea to keep an eye on the Family.

Unfortunately, Spahn made this suggestion within earshot of Lynette Fromme. Charlie Manson was paranoid enough on his own, so the last thing he needed was something to justify his paranoia. Nonetheless, he now had it. Donald "Shorty" Shea, Manson's one-time assailant and humiliator, was officially a problem for the Family.

In Manson's typical fashion, he would turn that problem into an opportunity.

CHAPTER SIX

"These children, everything they have done they have done for love of their brother . . . I have killed no one and I have ordered no one to be killed."
—CHARLES MANSON, COURT STATEMENT, NOVEMBER 19, 1970

Although Vincent Bugliosi's theory that Helter Skelter was the sole catalyst to the murders and the all-encompassing reason for all the paranoia, fear and control Manson exerted was overstated—the Helter Skelter theory was a very real concern on the ranch, at this point reaching a fever pitch.

Manson was variously worried about the Straight Satans because they wanted compensation for their bad mescaline, the Black Panthers avenging Bernard Crowe or the police stumbling across The Family's general operations. He had whipped all his followers into a frenzy and made them meticulously plan a retreat to the desert in the anticipation something would erupt any day and trigger Helter Skelter. The longer this went on, the more paranoid Charlie got.

The Family had taken to building dune buggies and slowly moving essential items to Barker Ranch. A few knew their time at Spahn was limited, but those who had been to Barker were not looking forward to setting up there. Living was a lot harder.

They could understand how going to the remote Barker Ranch would be necessary once Helter Skelter started. But when was that going to be? Manson kept promising it was imminent, but there was little signal of it and most of the Family were not smart enough or too naive to recognize what had to be done to start the Helter Skelter war.

"It was almost as though we had to make the first move for it to continue to develop, to get bigger so that it would happen because the black man loves us so much that he would be our slave and do everything we said," Leslie Van Houten would later tell her attorneys.

It is easy to see how, assuming Van Houten was accurately paraphrasing what Manson had filled her with, some of the remaining Family members would eventually be drawn to Aryan Nation members and other white supremacists.

Paul Watkins was even more direct, later telling documentary filmmaker Robert Hendrickson that Manson had described how the Family would "one day up in the mountains in Beverly Hills, just go in and have a bunch of mass murders, and that they would be so atrocious and there would be blood splattered all over everything, that people would be chopped into pieces with knives, and there would be things written on the walls in blood.

"And the white man would get all uptight about it and blame the nigger for it."

But there was a more immediate concern. Bobby Beausoleil was still in prison, and Charlie Manson, leader, magician, and prophet, had not managed to free him yet. If Manson could not protect Beausoleil, who else would he not be able to protect?

Manson again began to plot. As usual, though, his thoughts primarily focused on how to turn the situation to benefit himself. On August 6, 1969, he announced he was going on a recruitment run. He commandeered one of the Family's trucks and headed toward San Francisco.

That trip yielded three benefits. First, Manson recruited seventeen-year-old Stephanie Schram, a new Family member. Second, on August 7, he was stopped by a police officer and was given a ticket for operating a vehicle without a license. Manson signed the ticket using his own name—establishing that he was far from the Spahn Ranch. And finally, he had an idea for a distraction.

Manson returned to the Spahn Ranch with a revelation. It was time for Helter Skelter.

* * *

At the Spahn Ranch, on the night of August 8, 1969, Susan Atkins told Barbara Hoyt to go into the communal clothes pile and pull out three sets of dark clothing. Atkins could have gotten the clothes herself, but she prided herself on maintaining a certain level of respect and fear among the other female Family members.

It was, as it turned out, a pointless request. By the time Hoyt returned with the items, Atkins, Patricia Krenwinkel, and Charles Watson, along with driver Linda Kasabian, had already left for the night.

Kasabian had been a Family member for only a few weeks at this time, but was the only one with a valid driving license, something Charlie had deemed essential in case they got stopped by the cops.

She was likely a second choice. The other person at the ranch with a valid license, Mary Brunner, Manson's oldest and most loyal Family member, had been arrested earlier that evening, along with Sandra Good, for using a stolen credit card. The delivery van Manson had been driving during the past two days, which they had used, was now impounded. It may have given Manson an alibi, if there had not been a record of it being back in Los Angeles.

Good, who was close to her due date for the baby she was carrying, was soon released. She went straight back to Spahn. Brunner, on the other hand, was facing a separate charge for forgery, and would be kept in jail for close to a month.

But where were the four killers being driven to? During a plea hearing, Atkins would claim Manson believed he was sending the four to a place where Terry Melcher still lived. But Manson knew Melcher was in Malibu. He most likely told them to target Melcher in an attempt to motivate them to kill for revenge, which was easier than motivating them to kill randomly.

"The reason Charlie picked that house was to instill fear into Terry Melcher because Terry had given us his word on a few things and never came through with them," Atkins said. "So Charlie wanted to put some fear into him, let him know that what Charlie said was the way it is."

Always tell people what they are most interested in hearing, as the Dale Carnegie training says.

Manson had given a last instruction before the four drove off. He had leaned in the window and told the girls to leave a sign. Something "witchy."

But the killings were only part of the mission. Manson would occasionally talk about how women have "witchcraft"—attention to small details that underscore what is going on. It could mean little flourishes on clothing they sewed. It could mean adding an extra flavor to a soup. Or it could mean an extra touch of horror during a killing.

Tex Watson would later claim to be gripped by fear, pre-deed. "The night of the murders, I tried to medicate my pain with methamphetamines, but actually it made it easier to turn my rebellion, fear, and anger loose on my victims."

Whether he was truly doing it to mask his pain, or he was indulging in the drugs he habitually and almost daily ingested, is something only he knows. But according to most Manson Family members, most of their fears had been leached out of them by drugs and Manson's brainwashing techniques.

* * *

Late summer nights in Los Angeles are warm, but generally comfortable—the ocean breeze sees to that. The sun had set around eight o'clock, and the evening air was just cool enough to keep the windows open. It was a fine night for hanging out or running lazy errands, and eighteen-year-old Steven Parent was doing a little of both. A few weeks earlier, Parent had picked up a hitchhiking Bill Garretson, the nineteen-year-old houseboy and caretaker of a house at 10050 Cielo Drive. Now Parent had a clock radio he thought Garretson might like to buy. A little before midnight, Parent showed up at Garretson's small house behind the main residence.

Garretson did not want the clock radio, but was willing to share a Friday night beer with Parent. The company was a distraction from his not-too-strenuous work of caring for the house and grounds. The work was pretty easy, as the owner, Rudi Altobelli, had a laid-back approach. A previous tenant, Candice Bergen, had strung Christmas lights around the front of the estate. When she, her boyfriend Terry Melcher, and Mark Lindsay, the lead singer of Paul Revere and the Raiders, who had been living with them, moved out in January 1969, the lights stayed.

The house did not stay unoccupied for long. In February, filmmaker Roman Polanski and his pregnant wife, actress Sharon Tate, moved in, and Garretson had been brought on as a favor to them. But even they did not use the house constantly. Polanski was often jetting off to work on film projects, and Tate had her own activities. In their place, Abigail Folger and Wojciech Frykowski had been using one of the spare bedrooms. Tate had recently returned pending the birth of her son.

A little after midnight, Parent made a phone call to a friend—it would be the last phone call anyone would make from 10050 Cielo Drive that evening. Shortly after Parent hung up, Tex Watson scaled a telephone pole just outside the chain-link gates and cut the line. Then he, Susan Atkins, and Patricia Krenwinkel climbed over an embankment near the gate—they did not want to touch the actual gate, fearing it was electrified—and slipped into the darkness on the estate grounds to stash the changes of clothes they were carrying in the bushes. They left their driver, Kasabian, with the car.

Parent, having made plans to meet a friend, left Garretson and drove past the main house.

In the main house, Tate, Folger, Frykowski, and Sebring were enjoying a quiet evening. There was hashish and marijuana, and the male partiers might have taken a little MDA, a hallucinogenic stimulant. While Sebring had a gram of cocaine in his car, the vibe of the night was rather mellow. Folger and Tate were not interested in drugs, and Tate, at any rate, would have been wary of taking anything while pregnant.

Around 100 feet from the main house, Steven Parent's white AMC Rambler rolled to a stop in front of the closed gate of the estate. Parent leaned out of his window to punch the button that would grant him access.

Watson emerged from the shadows, carrying a substantial length of rope, a buck knife, and a .22 Buntline revolver—the same revolver Manson had used to shoot Bernard Lotsapoppa Crowe.

Parent had time to beg once—"Please don't hurt me, I won't tell anyone"— before Watson slashed Parent's wrist with the knife. Then Watson opened fire, hitting Parent four times and killing him.

Neither the people in the main house, nor Garretson in the back, heard anything. As Atkins would later say about the gunshots, " . . . they weren't that loud. It was a very quiet gun."

Watson, Atkins, and Krenwinkel pushed Parent's car further up the driveway so it would not be noticeable from the street. They then approached the main house, and Watson cut a screen window, slipped inside, and let Atkins and Krenwinkel in through the front door.

They first came upon Frykowski, who was sleeping on a couch in the living room. Tex woke Frykowski by standing in front of him and pointing a gun at him.

"I am the devil," Watkins announced. "I'm here to do the devil's business."

Watson sent Atkins to look for other residents while Krenwinkel stood by. Atkins came across Abigail Folger in one bedroom. The two smiled at each other—just a couple of visitors to this wonderful open house, yes?—and Atkins moved on to another bedroom, where she glimpsed Sebring, fully clothed, sitting on a bed. Tate was next to him on her back, clad in a bikini bra and panties, eight months pregnant. Tate and Polanski had already picked out a name for their soon-to-be-born son: Paul Richard Polanski. Neither Tate nor Sebring saw Atkins, who went back to Watson for instructions.

Watson told her to tie Sebring up. He then told Atkins to bring Folger to the living room. Again, Atkins walked to Folger's bedroom, but this time she entered and waved a knife in front of her.

"Go out in the living room," Atkins said. "Don't ask any questions."

There were no questions. People in shock usually cannot ask any.

Atkins turned Folger over to the other two, and went to fetch Sebring and Tate. Like the others, they were too stunned to resist. Both were brought to the living room.

Watson told Sebring, Folger, and Tate to lie on the floor, face down. It was then Sebring made the one gallant, heroic move of the evening. Still standing, Sebring gestured at Tate. "Can't you see she's pregnant? Let her sit down!"

Watson, the former high school honor student, college fraternity member, and student athlete, immediately shot him.

Folger and Tate screamed. Watson told them to be quiet and demanded money. Folger offered seventy-two dollars she had in her bedroom. She and Atkins fetched it and returned to the living room.

That money would not be enough to buy their escape. No amount would.

Frykowski was trying. He had loosened the restraints Krenwinkel had tied around his hands. A second attempt by Atkins, in which she used a towel, was no more successful, but the Manson crew did not realize it.

Watson looped the rope he had brought around Sebring's neck, then around Folger and Tate's necks. He tossed the rope over a ceiling beam and pulled on it. The tug forced Folger and Tate to stand, Tate rising in an ungainly manner. Not to do so would have meant they'd be strangled. Sebring may or may not have been conscious. He may or may not have been alive. He was definitely in no condition to resist.

Grasping for a last thread of hope, one of the victims asked, "What are you going to do with us?"

Watson's answer was cold: "You are all going to die." He then told Atkins to kill Frykowski.

By this time, however, Frykowski had wriggled free of Atkins's ineptly tied bonds. When she moved to him, he grabbed her, knocking her down. The two were fighting, each knowing the loser would die.

Frykowski might have had a size advantage, but Susan had a knife. As Frykowski grabbed her she swung wildly, hitting his leg. Frykowski let go of her and bolted for the front door, screaming for help.

Watson intercepted Frykowski, smashing him repeatedly over the head with the butt of his gun while frantically stabbing. The coroner's report would later find Frykowski had been shot twice, bludgeoned thirteen times, and stabbed fifty-one times.

While the killers' attention was turned to Frykowski, Folger had managed to loosen the rope around her neck and had grabbed Krenwinkel. Tate, meanwhile, was struggling with her ropes.

Frykowski getting away would have been bad, but losing a Family member would have been worse. Watson left Frykowski to help Krenwinkel subdue Folger. As Watson raised his knife, Folger dropped her arms, looked at her assailants, and slumped.

"You've got me," Folger said. "I give up."

Watson stabbed her in the belly, and she fell to the floor.

Sharon Tate, despite her advanced pregnancy, was struggling, if not fighting. Defensive injuries suggest the latter. She, too, was trying to pull the rope from around her neck. But Atkins was determined to claim at least one victim with a minimum of resistance. She forced Tate to the living room couch as Tate begged for her life, and the life of her baby.

And then Atkins said the words that almost certainly would condemn her to the gas chamber.

"Woman, I have no mercy for you."

By this time, Frykowski had managed to stagger and crawl out the front door. Watson bolted after him. Frykowski did not get very far. Whether from the wounds he had already sustained or from the final assaults from Watson, he did not make it much past the door, especially after Watson hit him on the head several times with his gun's butt, breaking the handle.

Watson's little errand, tying up the loose end that was Frykowski, did not take much time. He returned to find Atkins and Tate in a tableau of pleading and psychosis. Atkins and Watson both stabbed her, with Watson delivering a thrust to Tate's heart that caused her to fall from the couch to the floor.

That was where detectives would find her.

Atkins would later claim she had wanted to cut Tate's baby out of her womb, but there had not been time. Instead, she would content herself with tasting Tate's blood.

Sebring was collapsed near the fireplace. Tate had crumpled at the foot of the couch, her left hand clutching her chest, the other arm thrown casually across her forehead as if she were napping . . . except that the running wounds in her chest, cheek, and elsewhere were covering her with blood.

Frykowski's body was already cooling on the front lawn. Folger had been badly hurt, but she had one last reserve of desire to live inside her. She ran through the back door, past the pool, out onto the lawn, and headed toward the split-rail fence that lined the property. She was running blind; she did not head toward the gate, instead fleeing right as she ran.

Watson and the two girls went after her. It was not much of a chase. By the time Watson reached her near a fir tree she was already down. Watson stabbed her a handful of times, just to make sure.

When detectives first saw Folger's body, the white nightgown she was wearing was so soaked with blood that they swore it was red. The coroner said she had been stabbed twenty-eight times.

Manson's team was not done playing with the bodies, however. Watson wanted Atkins to leave a sign hinting at impending terror.

Atkins re-entered the house. She saw the towel she had used to unsuccessfully bind Frykowski's hands. She heard gurgling noises from Sharon Tate's body. She

An early promotional shot of Sharon Tate dating from around 1967. (The Mega Agency)

Sharon Tate and Roman Polanski photographed as they leave church on their wedding day, January 20, 1968, in London, UK. (The Mega Agency)

Bodies are removed from 10050 Cielo Drive after the Manson Family murders. (Police handout, public domain)

The bodies of Victims Abigail Folger and Wojciech Frykowski were found on the lawn outside the house, while Steven Parent was found in his car on the driveway. (Police handout, public domain)

A driving license, possibly fake or altered, belonging to Charles Manson, expiring in 1969.

A picture of Susan Atkins taken from the 1965 yearbook for Leigh High School in San Jose, California.

A mugshot of Charles Manson from 1968, reportedly taken while he was high on acid.

A mugshot of Charles Tex Watson from 1969.

BK 728129009096
LOS ANGELES
POLICE

A mugshot of Susan Atkins taken circa 1969.

A mugshot of Bobby Beausoleil after his arrest for the murder of Gary Hinman in 1969.

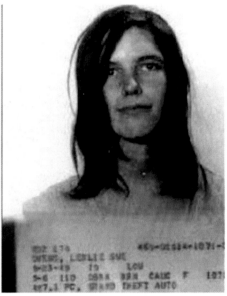

Mugshot of Leslie Van Houten, pictured in an official police evidence photograph.

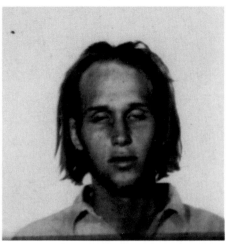

Mugshot of Manson Family member Steve Grogan.

Mugshot of Patricia Krenwinkle.

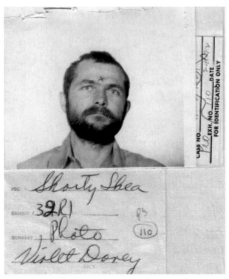

Mugshot of Bruce Davis, submitted as evidence in the murder of Donald "Shorty" Shea.

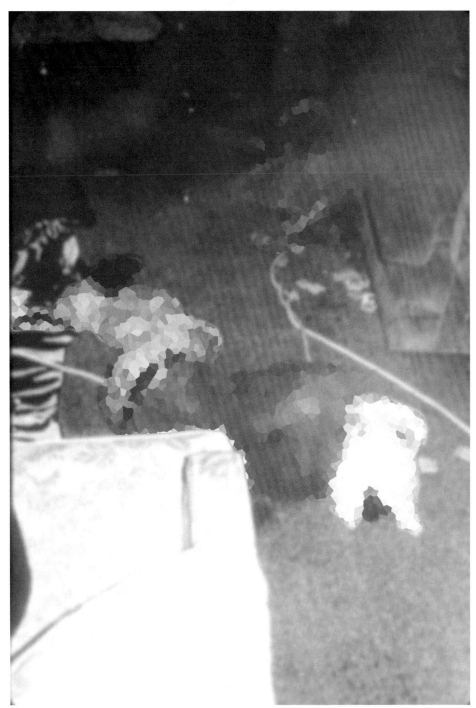

The body of Jay Sebring and eight-month pregnant Sharon Tate in the living room of 10050 Cielo Drive in Los Angeles. They both had ropes tied around their necks and were stabbed to death by the Manson Family—along with three others—on August 8, 1969. (Police evidence photo, public domain)

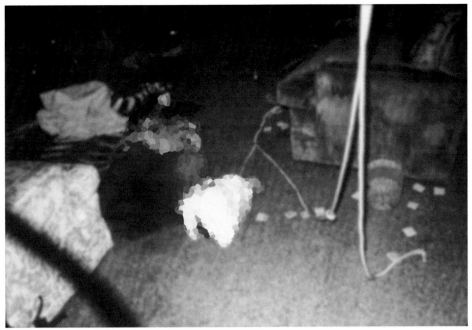

A police evidence photo showing the corpse of Jay Sebring on the floor of the living room at 10050 Cielo Drive in Los Angeles, after he was murdered by the Manson Family on August 8, 1969. (Police evidence photo, public domain)

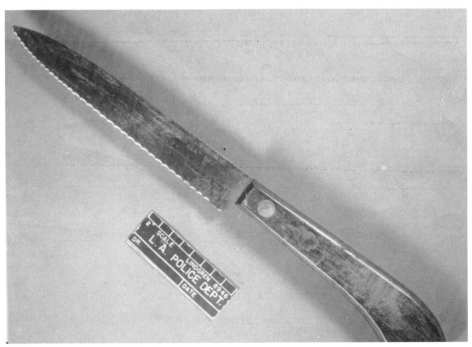

One of the knives used in the murders at the Tate residence. (Police evidence photo, public domain)

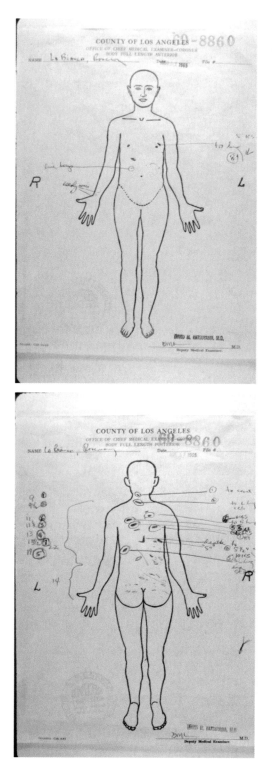

A Los Angeles County Medical Examiner's card detailing the wounds inflicted on Rosemary LaBianca, who was murdered in her home in Los Angeles by the Manson Family on August 9, 1969. (Los Angeles County Chief Medical Examiner)

A Los Angeles County Medical Examiner's card detailing the wounds inflicted on Leno LaBianca, who was murdered in his home in Los Angeles by the Manson Family on August 9, 1969. (Los Angeles County Chief Medical Examiner)

CASE NO. 69-8796   NAME: SHARON TATE POLANSKI

DOCUMENTED WOUNDS	STAB	GSW	Incised Wounds	
Chest	4			#1, 2, 3, 4
Abdomen	1			#5
Back	8			#5, 6, 7, 8, 9, 10, 11, 12
Arm – right upper	1			#14 (Through and through)
Arm – left upper	1			#15
Thigh-right-back	1			#16
Arm – left forearm			2	
TOTAL DOCUMENTED	16		2	

SUMMARY OF WOUNDS: 16 stab wounds
                            2 incised wounds

FATAL WOUNDS: #1, #2, #3

WOUNDS NOT DOCUMENTED: All wounds documented

NOTE: Duplication of the number 5: 1 in abdomen, 1 in back
         (Both wounds numbered 5)

NOTE: The number 13 was omitted

SHARON TATE POLANSKI

REVIEW OF STAB WOUNDS

NO.	LOCATION		DIRECTION	SIZE	DEEP	PENETRATED	SERIOUSNESS FATALITY
1	↑ C H E S T ↓	Left pericardial area	Left → Right 45°	1-1/2"	4"	4th ICS, pericardium, heart	Fatal
2		Left Chest	Left → Right	1-3/4"	4"	4th ICS, pericardium, heart	Fatal
3		Left lower chest	Left → Right	1-1/2"	4"	6th Rib, Heart	Fatal
4		Left breast		1"	3"		
5	Abdomen	Left breast	Left → Right Horizontal	1"	4"-5"	Liver	Potentially Fatal
6	↓ B A C K	Scapula, left Upper back	Horizontal	1"	2"		
7		Left paravertebral	Horizontal	1"	3"	Left lung	Potentially Fatal
8		Left lower scapula	Horizontal	1"	2 1/4"		
9	- - -	Right mid scapula line	Horizontal	1"	3"	Right lung	Potentially Fatal
10	C H E S T	Left lower thoracic	Horizontal	1"	2"	Deep muscle	
11		Left lower thoracic	Horizontal	1"	3"	Left lung	Potentially Fatal
12		Left paravertebral	Horizontal	1"	2"	Deeper muscle	
#5 (13)	Area	Mid line	Horizontal	1"	2"	Deeper muscle	
14	Right Upper Arm	Through and through wound, lateral aspect mid upper arm		1-1/2"→1"	5"	R Biceps M	
15	L.Upper Arm			1-1/4"	1-1/2"	L Biceps M	
16	R.Thigh	Lateral lower thigh	Upward	3/4"	2-1/2"		Superficial
I 1-2	Lt. Arm	Left forearm		3/4"	1/2"		

Hemothorax – Right   500 cc.

A Los Angeles County Medical Examiner's report cards detailing the wounds inflicted on Sharon Tate after examining her body following her murder by the Manson Family on August 8, 1969. (Los Angeles County Chief Medical Examiner)

Left: Charles Manson is cuffed and led to court in Inyo County, California wearing a prison-issue jumpsuit in a photo taken on December 3, 1969, on charges of arson and receiving stolen goods. At that time he was also indicted on the murders of Sharon Tate and four others. (The Mega Agency)

Right and Below: Charles Manson led away from court in Inyo County, California. By this time the media were branding him a "hippy cult leader" and linking him to the Tate murders. (The Mega Agency)

Charles Manson in the chapel at the California Medical Facility in Vacaville in 1980. The murderer was at the prison from 1976 to 1985 for psychiatric treatment. (The Mega Agency)

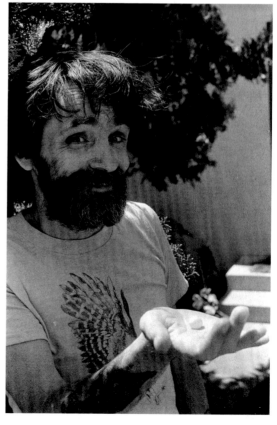

Charles Manson shows an open palm and cracks a smile in a picture taken at the California Medical Facility in Vacaville, 1980. (The Mega Agency)

Charles Manson poses with a guitar and a piano at the California Medical Facility in Vacaville, 1980. (The Mega Agency)

Charles Manson gives a trademark evil stare as he is pictured at the California Medical Facility in Vacaville, 1980. (The Mega Agency)

Charles Manson pictured on January 25, 1971, being led away from court after being found guilty of the Tate-LaBianca murders. (The Mega Agency)

Manson Family member Susan Atkins is pictured at an arraignment in the Sharon Tate murder case at Los Angeles Superior Court on January 15, 1970. Photographers were blocked off from the defendants as they were led into court. (The Mega Agency)

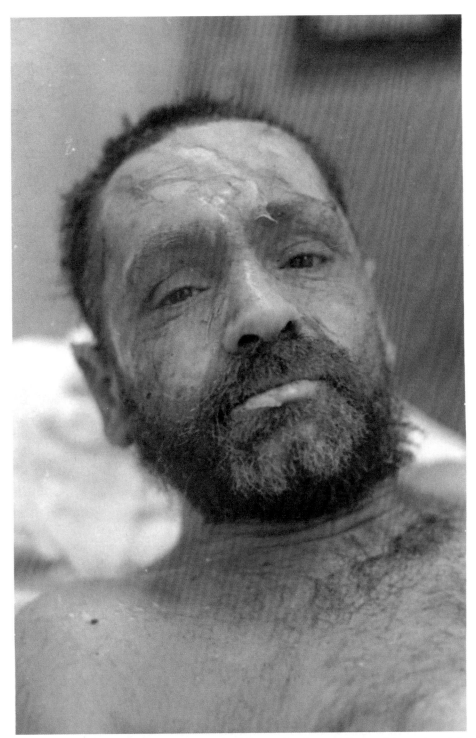

Charles Manson displays his burned face after being doused in paint thinner and set alight at California Medical Facility. He was attacked by Jan Holmstrom over an argument about his Hare Krishna religious beliefs.

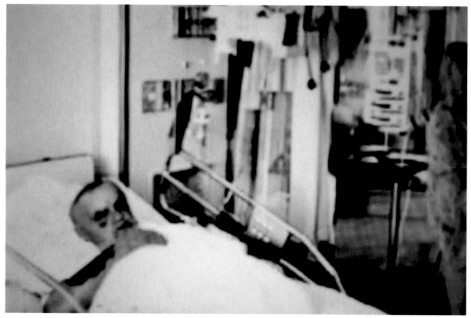

Bruised and with his health failing, this is the last known photo of Charles Manson alive taken in the hospital just days before his death on November 19, 2017.

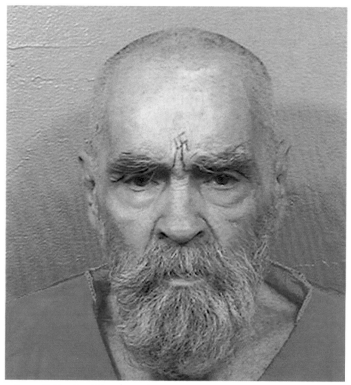

The last mugshot of Charles Manson taken on August 14, 2017, three months before his death. (California Department of Corrections)

remembered seeing "political piggy" written on the wall of Gary Hinman's apartment.

Using the towel, Atkins carefully printed "PIG" on the front door of 10050 Cielo Drive in Sharon Tate's blood. She then tossed the bloody towel back into the house. It landed on Sebring's head, covering it. Atkins, who had already turned to leave, would not know this until the trial.

The three headed toward the estate's entrance. They scooped up the changes of clothing they had left in the bushes. Watson pressed the button to open the gate—the one Steven Parent never had a chance to push. Watson did not realize he was leaving a bloody fingerprint on the gate button, and neither did one of the investigators who would later press the button himself, re-opening the gate for other vehicles and simultaneously obscuring a piece of evidence.

Atkins, Krenwinkel, and Watson walked through the entrance and down a hill, to where Linda Kasabian was waiting in their car. Atkins was fussing. She could not find the buck knife she'd brought with her, and feared she had left it in the house, but was unwilling to go back inside.

The three killers changed their clothes and bundled up their bloody garments. Kasabian soon stopped the car atop a roadside hill and they tossed the bloody clothes over the side.

The three may have been wearing clean clothes, but they still had telltale gore on their skin. They stopped at a house on a side street—a bit of craftiness to avoid witnesses—and used a garden hose to rinse.

They were, perhaps, as inept about doing so undetected as they had been about coordinating their murders. Almost immediately, the couple who owned the home detected their presence and chased them away.

Who knows what would have happened to those homeowners if the Family members still had murder on their minds?

They arrived back at the Spahn Ranch roughly two hours after they had left.

* * *

The house at 10050 Cielo Drive was quiet when housekeeper Winifred Chapman arrived shortly after 8 a.m. on Saturday morning. She saw the cut phone line and was worried, but the electric gate, at least, was still working. She was late, and hurried up the driveway past several cars—including Steven Parent's Rambler, with Parent's body still in it. The car had been pushed off to the side.

Within minutes, Chapman was running back down the driveway, far, far faster than when she arrived. This time, she ran as if demons were behind her.

She may not have been wrong.

* * *

Charlie Manson was not happy.

The murders at the Tate house had been incredibly sloppy. As the deeds were described by those who had gone to the house, there was too much mess, and too much panic.

By some accounts, Manson and Nancy Pitman supposedly drove to 10050 Cielo Drive after the killers returned to Spahn Ranch to inspect their work. It seems farfetched and, if true, was incredibly foolish. Manson claimed he went back to clear up the crime scene, but criminals returning to the scene of a crime doubles the risk of getting caught and it would add risk for himself of leaving evidence and becoming implicated in the crimes—which seemed to be the opposite of his intention.

Either way, Manson was not impressed. If the murders had been intended to trigger the racial war of his philosophies, or if they had been meant to throw a targeted scare into Terry Melcher, from Family member descriptions it did not sound as though the clues were there for the straight society, the "pigs," or the black community to pick up on.

The early news reports confirmed Manson's fears. *Tragedy! Slaughter! Four beautiful people struck down in their prime! Blonde starlet's baby ripped from her womb!* The papers were not above a little disinformation of their own.

No mention of an impending race war. No blame assigned to black people. No rioting in the streets. No lit fuse for Helter Skelter.

And the seventy-two dollars taken from Abigail Folger was not going to help with the Family's financial needs.

Not everyone was displeased with how the evening had turned out. Barbara Hoyt, who had been told to pick out dark clothing for three people the night before, observed some Family members slipping off to watch one of the few televisions on the Spahn Ranch, all in the rooms of non-Family folks. She saw some of them reacting with glee to reports of the Tate murders.

Strange.

Faced with circumstances like those now confronting Manson, an aspiring messiah has two choices: blame himself or blame the apostles.

Manson, of course, turned his frustration at the Helter Skelter message around to anger at the participants. Helter Skelter was so imminent, so powerful, so *now* that once revealed, it could not be ignored. Clearly, it had not been revealed by the messages left at 10050 Cielo Drive. The Family had failed him.

The next night, August 9, 1969, Saturday night into Sunday morning, the Family would have to try again. And Charlie Manson, leader of a murderous cult, catalyst for Helter Skelter, and perhaps—just perhaps—alibi seeker for the imprisoned Bobby Beausoleil, was going to show the world, or at least his followers, how to do things the right way.

Manson wanted new participants to join in the next murders. And he wanted to make sure that whoever he chose would meet his standards for correct procedures—whatever they were.

Watson, of course, would have to go. A man needed to be present for this type of work, not just physically but psychologically, according to Manson's worldview. And Krenwinkel, who had left the first messages, had to go again because the signs left behind in blood would have to match.

But Manson wanted Linda Kasabian and Susan Atkins, accompanied by token man Clem Grogan, to go on another job. They were to track down and kill Saladin Nader, a Lebanese actor Kasabian had recently met while she and Sandra Good had been hitchhiking. The three had gone back to his apartment, where Good fell asleep and Kasabian and the man had sex. He was, Kasabian thought, nice.

Manson would not have cared about that. He would have been more concerned that Kasabian, and whoever she was with, would be able to get into Nader's apartment without much fuss.

Manson wanted another woman for the LaBianca break-in. On the night of Saturday, August 9, he pulled aside Leslie Van Houten and posed to her a very important question:

"Are you crazy?" Manson asked.

"Well, yeah," replied Van Houten.

She knew what Manson meant. Was she crazy enough to believe what he believed, to see things the way he saw them, and that it was necessary for the Family to do whatever it took to start Helter Skelter? That *she* could do it?

Yes, she was crazy.

An approving Manson told her to find two changes of clothing and go to the 1959 Ford owned by a Spahn ranch-hand, where other Family members were waiting.

Not just Van Houten, but the passenger capability of the yellow car was going to be tested and taxed that night. Kasabian would be at the wheel, and Atkins, Grogan, Van Houten, Krenwinkel, Manson, Watson, and their various changes of clothing squeezed themselves into the front and back seats.

Catherine Gillies saw the Family members gathered at the Ford, and had a pretty good idea of what they were up to. She approached the group and asked if she could join. No, she was told, the car could only fit so many.

This justification was only partly true. Van Houten would later say that Gillies's habit of occasionally vanishing from the Spahn Ranch had kept her out of the circle of trust needed to be a Family murderer.

In the car, Manson directed and Kasabian drove. Saturday turned to Sunday. Manson put on a good show about looking for just the right random house, even at one point stopping the car, getting out, and looking in a window.

When he returned to the car and crushed his way in, he told the other occupants, "Man, there were pictures of children in that house. I just couldn't do that."

They wound up at Harold True's house on Waverly Drive, although driver Kasabian, who had only been with the Family for a month, could not have known that. Some of the others in the car, including Atkins, recognized it, however. Family members had visited it three times during the previous year. Manson, who had slipped into it to escape the noise of Harold True's party and perhaps lie down with one or more of its guests, would have been able to provide a rough interior layout.

Manson ordered the other six Family members to wait in the car and disappeared into the darkness. They did as they were told. When Manson returned, he motioned for Watson to join him. Manson was armed with a pistol and Watson carried a bayonet.

The two quietly entered through the unlocked back door of the house and approached Leno LaBianca, who was asleep on a couch in the living room. Leno woke to find Manson pointing the pistol at him. Manson quietly assured Leno that he was there to rob the house, and that if he cooperated he would take what he wanted and leave without hurting anyone.

Manson told Leno to lie on his stomach on the couch. Manson then bound him, improvising bonds from the long, strong leather thong the killer wore around his own neck.

Manson then asked whether anyone else was in the house. Leno answered in the affirmative. Upon hearing that Leno's wife Rosemary had gone to bed, Manson sent Watson to fetch her. Watson also grabbed her wallet.

Manson's part in the murders was almost done. While Watson watched the LaBiancas, Manson pulled Krenwinkel and Van Houten from the waiting Ford and brought them into the house.

Van Houten noticed that both Rosemary and Leno tensed upon their arrival. They had to realize, once the two girls walked in, that this was not going to be just a robbery.

Watson was armed with a bayonet. The girls did not have weapons, so they went into the LaBiancas' kitchen and selected a couple of knives.

The Family members who had been at the Tate killing had described their victims' panicked last efforts once they saw each other start to be butchered. Manson was not going to let there be a replay of that. He told Krenwinkel and Van Houten to move Rosemary into the bedroom. His plan was to kill the LaBiancas simultaneously.

Once the women were out of earshot, Manson went to Watson to give a few last instructions, which included telling the three to hitchhike to the Spahn Ranch. And Manson had one last order.

"Make sure everyone does something," he said.

Then he was gone.

Krenwinkel and Van Houten took Rosemary into the bedroom and sat her on the bed. They covered her head with a pillowcase which they secured with a lamp cord. While the woman sucked hard breaths through the fabric, the killers, all the while, assured her she would be okay. Watson, who had grabbed a pillowcase from the bedroom, was doing the same with Leno in the living room. When Watson tied his lamp cord, it was tight enough to start cutting off Leno's breathing.

Leno was already struggling before his death began in earnest. Watson struck first. He thrust his bayonet into Leno's throat, but it was not enough to stop him, even though he was bound, from writhing, twisting, and crying out.

At that, Rosemary jumped up, managed to grab a lampshade, and started swinging it at Van Houten.

"What are you doing to my husband?" the doomed woman screamed. "What are you doing to my husband?"

Watson was doing to Leno what Krenwinkel and Van Houten were trying to do to her. But there was a problem. Krenwinkel was struggling with the knives the girls had grabbed from the kitchen. They were flimsy, and rather than piercing Rosemary's body, as Krenwinkel stabbed her collarbone, they bent.

"Tex!"—meaning Watson—Van Houten yelled. "We can't kill her!"

It was not for lack of trying. Krenwinkel had finally managed to break flesh with some of her thrusts, and Rosemary was badly wounded. But she fought with the desperation of the condemned and Watson, who by now had joined the girls, finished the job with his sturdy bayonet.

Van Houten had initially—unsuccessfully—tried to hold Rosemary while Krenwinkel stabbed her, and had stepped aside when Watson finished the job. Had she stabbed Rosemary herself? Neither Krenwinkel nor Watson could be sure, even though Watson had his orders from Manson that everyone was to participate in the killings.

Rosemary was face-down on the floor. Van Houten crouched beside her with a knife in her hand and began stabbing blindly. The coroner would report that Rosemary had forty-one stab wounds, many of which seemed to have been made after she was dead. There were sixteen in her back and buttocks, most of which had been Van Houten's gruesome handiwork. There was blood, and a lot of it, but there might have been more had Rosemary LaBianca not bled internally as well as externally. As one detective later put it, "She drowned in her own blood."

Krenwinkel was busy doing something witchy. She had sopped up some of Leno's blood from the twenty-six stab wounds and fourteen punctures he had suffered with a rag. Just as the Family had done in the Hinman and Tate killings, she was industriously writing on the living room walls. She smeared the words "Death to pigs" above a series of framed pictures and certificates. "Rise" appeared high next to a door frame. And in the kitchen, on the refrigerator door, she mis-spelled the reason for the two days of slaughter: "Helter Skelter."

Watson, meanwhile, was cutting the word WAR into Leno's belly in large, straight slashes.

As a finishing touch, Krenwinkel stuck a carving fork in his stomach and a steak knife in his throat, intending a nod to The Beatles' song "Piggies." When she was done, she tapped the fork and watched it wobble.

Krenwinkel, Watson, and Van Houten snacked on the LaBiancas' food as they worked; Watson took a shower as the girls began wiping their fingerprints from various surfaces.

There were no apparent bloodstains on the dark clothes the three wore. When they left, they hitchhiked most of the way back to Spahn Ranch. According to Van Houten, they gratefully bought breakfast for one of the men who picked them up.

* * *

It's easy to imagine Kasabian cursing the day she passed her driver's-ed test.

She had been the wheelman the night of the Tate killings, which had been bad enough when she did not know exactly what was going on. She had thought, based on the fact that Krenwinkel, Van Houten, and Watson were all carrying dark clothing, that they were going on just another creepy crawl. A night later, she was driving Family members again—and this time, she had a pretty good idea what their plans were.

When Manson returned to the car, he handed Kasabian the wallet he had taken from Rosemary LaBianca. At his order she took all the cash out of it and wiped fingerprints off—his, at least.

Manson then told her to drive to a black neighborhood, where they would leave the wallet for a black person to find. That person would use the credit cards and be implicated for the LaBianca murders. And the Tate murders. And, hopefully, the killing of Gary Hinman.

Helter Skelter.

As dubious as the plan was, Manson once again over-thought it and sabotaged the crime. Someone might have found the wallet and used the credit cards *if* he had Kasabian throw the wallet out the window as originally planned. But Manson had a better idea. What if Kasabian took it into a ladies' room at a gas station and left it there? It is difficult to imagine what he thought that would do, other than to possibly send investigators off in the wrong direction.

Kasabian said she would. And when they found a gas station she walked into the ladies' room, took the top off the toilet tank, and dropped the wallet in. She replaced the top of the tank, composed herself, and left.

It was her first act of rebellion that night.

Manson then told her to go to the apartment complex where Saladin Nader lived. Manson had never met Nader, but a few days before, while Kasabian and Sandra Good were in Venice, Nader had picked the two of them up and had sex with Kasabian.

Was the sex good? Manson wanted to know. *Might Nader want another little party? Did Kasabian think she could get into his apartment?*

Yes and yes and yes, Linda said. Then Manson handed Kasabian a knife, and explained exactly what he expected of her. Another killing of another pig, with appropriate writing on the wall.

Kasabian was terrified.

"I'm not you, Charlie," she said. "I can't kill anyone."

Manson's standard response to a flat-out refusal of his will, the few times when it happened, was a beating. But the four were in public and not the relative isolation of the Spahn Ranch. As so, a physical rebuke would have attracted attention. It also would have taken the focus off the task at hand.

Kasabian would have gladly taken a beating instead of having to go through with a murder, but Manson was not going to let her get away so easily. He had her indicate the apartment where Nader lived. And then he sent her, Atkins, and Grogan—because he felt women always need to be led by a man, even one nicknamed Scramblehead—to complete their tasks.

Then, once again, Charlie Manson drove away before any killing happened. He had no more idea that Kasabian had just done her third act of rebellion for the evening, any more than he suspected the other two.

She had indicated the wrong apartment.

The three approached the front door. Grogan and Atkins hung back slightly, armed and waiting for Kasabian to get entry into the apartment. When the bewildered occupant opened the door, he did not, of course, recognize Kasabian. Of course, there was no chance of getting into that apartment. Kasabian apologized for the interruption and excused herself, preventing any further killing that night—that we know of.

Grogan was too dumb not to be hoodwinked, but he would soon get his chance at murder. Atkins was not dumb, just sociopathic: denied a chance to kill, she shit in a stairwell as the three left the building.

The three hitchhiked back to Spahn Ranch, but upon arriving back found no sign of Manson.

Two days later, Manson instructed Kasabian to visit Bobby Beausoleil, Mary Brunner, and Sandy Good in jail, where the three were awaiting trial for the murder of Gary Hinman. Rather than complete her errand, Kasabian, who was pregnant with her second child, slipped off to join her husband in New Mexico, leaving her first child—daughter Tanya, then only just over a year old—with the Family. She trusted—hoped—the Family's philosophy about children, combined with the communal parenting, would keep her daughter safe.

While the two initially talked about rescuing their daughter, they determined doing so would be too dangerous. They would have to trust their daughter to the good intentions of a bloodthirsty Family of thrill-killing maniacs.

* * *

If Charlie Manson wanted chaos, all he would have had to do was visit 10050 Cielo Drive on the day the bodies were discovered.

The media had been on the scene even before some of the cops showed up. They jammed the entryway to the estate, blocking the driveway all the way down Cielo Drive. Police set up a perimeter to keep the area clear and the crime scene as uncontaminated as possible.

However, the first act by police on the scene was to press the button for the electric gate, obscuring the bloody fingerprint left by Tex Watson.

The chaos did not end at the bottom of the driveway of the murder scene. Right around the time Sharon Tate was being autopsied, a call came into the Los Angeles Police Department's homicide division from the Los Angeles County Sheriff's Department. Police there had seen the television footage from Cielo Drive. They were holding a kid named Bobby Beausoleil for murder. His victim's blood had been used to smear the words POLITICAL PIGGY on a wall.

Jess Buckles, an investigator temporarily assigned to the department while another detective was on vacation, did not see a connection. He did not bother mentioning the call to any of the other detectives.

In a sick way, the call vindicated Manson. The cops, at least, had a chance to link the crimes, albeit not to the Black Panthers. They chose to ignore that option. Similarly, the LaBianca murders were dismissed as copycat murders. In fact, the two sets of homicides were assigned to different detective teams. Their lack of communication added weeks to the time it took to start connecting the dots and get on top of the cases.

Part of the reason the police may not initially have been as aggressive about pursuing seemingly unrelated leads is that they had a likely suspect already in custody. William Garretson, the caretaker of the estate, who had been staying in one of the cottages well behind the main house, had been arrested almost immediately. Police found it suspicious that Garretson claimed not to have heard anything during the murders.

"I escaped death, and now I was going to be tried for something I didn't do," Garretson later said.

He was never charged, and was cleared after taking a lie detector test, being released on August 11.

Manson might have also taken a little comfort in knowing that citizens of Los Angeles, especially its entertainment class, were thrown into a panic. By the end of the weekend, gun sales throughout the city had skyrocketed. Additionally, the cost for highly trained guard dogs tripled to around $1,500—more than $10,000 in 2019 dollars.

Rumors floated through the halls of law enforcement and the hills of Hollywood about the Tate murders. The killer was a drug dealer. It was someone who one of the dead had sexually abused. It was a "rough trade" prostitute someone in the group—or perhaps even all of them, those profligate rich!—had picked up on the Sunset Strip. It was a known associate of the group who had taken some bad speed.

The victims were described in various levels of semi- or undress. The more lurid the rumor, it seemed, the more likely to fit the jet-setting narrative of the victims.

The presence of drugs—mostly Sebring's and Frykowski's—at the crime scene led celebrities who might have any connection to the victims to get rid of their own stashes. As one Hollywood figure told *Life* magazine, "Toilets are flushing all over Beverly Hills; the entire Los Angeles sewer system is stoned."

Among the wackier of the speculations was one by Ed George, a former prison guard at San Quentin and the California Medical Facility who claimed to have spoken several times with Manson while the fiend was finally incarcerated for good. According to George, Manson was a fierce environmentalist whose sole reason for killing Sharon Tate was because the house at 10050 Cielo Drive featured a patio made from endangered redwood trees.

The Tate killings hit closer to home for some celebrities than others. Steve McQueen had met Tate on the set of *The Cincinnati Kid* (1965) before she was replaced by Tuesday Weld. McQueen also knew—and was a client of—Jay Sebring. He was so shaken by the killings that he took to carrying a gun everywhere, including to Sebring's funeral.

Warren Beatty, who was not far removed from his Oscar-nominated performance as the gleeful killer Clyde Barrow in *Bonnie and Clyde* (1967), had known all four people murdered at 10050 Cielo Drive. He would soon contribute to a fund that promised $25,000 for information that led to the Tate killers.

Beatty later noted that, as the killings went unsolved, "the collective response to these killings was what you might expect if a small nuclear device had gone off."

For once, Hollywood's self-centeredness may not have been completely unfounded. Atkins, who would eventually be jailed on a separate charge, would later describe to a fellow prison inmate the Family's plans to kill a handful of

A-list celebrities. According to trial testimony by Virginia Graham, Atkins planned to castrate the famously virile Richard Burton and gouge out Elizabeth Taylor's signature violet eyes—but only after she had heated her knife and pressed it to her face.

Atkins also described special punishments for crooners who might compete with Manson, such as Tom Jones (having sex with him at knifepoint and then cutting his throat) and Frank Sinatra (suspending him upside down from a meat hook, skinning him alive while playing his music in the background, then tanning his flesh and turning it into purses). Just slashing the throat of Ol' Blue Eyes would not have been inventive enough; it had already been done in the film *The Joker is Wild* twelve years before. The Family took pride in being bloody killers. They would not, however, have wanted Manson to tell them they were unoriginal.

While some of these scenarios sound like jailhouse bragging, there is no question that after the Tate killings Manson instantly grasped the newsworthy benefits of slaughtering celebrities. There may well have been conversations about specific targets with the Family. The ideas put forth said as much for the individual fetishes and kink of Family members as they did for the master plan itself.

The LaBiancas, despite not traveling in the same glamorous circles as the first night's victims, generated their own set of rumors. It was suggested that Leno, who was known to be a gambler, was a victim of any one of the bookies he had stiffed. He served on the board of a bank that supposedly had ties to the Mafia— this was obviously *their* doing. Rosemary had once ripped off an ex-husband and he had finally taken his revenge.

The police had decided there was no link between the killings. The newspapers—especially some of the tabloids—felt otherwise, and played up the two sets of murders as linked in a series of ritual killings.

The only victim who did not spawn a series of lurid theories was Steven Parent, the eighteen-year-old who had been leaving the Tate estate after unsuccessfully trying to sell his clock radio. There is not much in the way of conspiracies that can be generated about an eighteen-year-old stereo equipment enthusiast who had graduated high school two months before his murder.

In a very obvious way, a lot of the speculation was Hollywood being Hollywood. In the first eight months of 1969, the film industry had upped the body count in its output and poured on the blood in films such as *Where Eagles Dare* (with Richard Burton) and the already infamous, slow-motion violence of *The Wild Bunch*. Even the once-bloodless John Wayne was gunning enemies into the ground in the hard-riding *True Grit*. They had willfully championed counterculture, drug-fueled rebellion in *Easy Rider*, and open, sleazy sex in *Midnight Cowboy*.

The minds and imaginations of filmmakers were simply doing what they had always done: merging storylines to explain the killings. It was *The Lodger* meets *Key Largo*, but with an X rating. The decades-old debate about whether Hollywood actually inspired violence was muted for now, presumably out of respect for the dead. But it was quietly present.

And those whispered concerns changed absolutely nothing. Almost a year to the day after the Tate murders, the incredibly violent, gory *Soldier Blue* hit theaters. The following year, for all their artistic merits, it was *A Clockwork Orange*. A year later, *The Godfather*. The debate about the influence of violent media continued...along with increasingly violent films.

CHAPTER SEVEN

"I knew a guy that used to work in the stockyards and he used to kill cows all day long with a big sledgehammer, and then go home at night and eat dinner with his children and eat the meat that he slaughtered. Then he would go to church and read the Bible, and he would say, 'That is not killing.' And I look at him and I say, 'That doesn't make any sense, what are you talking about?'"

—CHARLES MANSON, COURT STATEMENT, NOVEMBER 19, 1970

According to Charlie, Helter Skelter was closer than ever.

The Family was instructed to focus on its preparations. The mechanics—heck, anyone who could tighten a lug nut or help lift an engine block—were converting any vehicles they could into dune buggies, the better to negotiate the rough terrain at Barker Ranch.

Family members had been doing so all along, but now there was an intensity to their work. When Barbara Hoyt first joined the Family in the spring of 1969, she had been enthused about their automotive work, even against the backdrop of an impending race war.

"They were building dune buggies with fur seats and gun mounts," Hoyt would later say. "They were making clothes out of hides. It was like they were all pioneers. I thought, 'Wow! This is fun. It's like camping.'"

The activities remained the same, but the mood changed after the Tate/LaBianca murders. Manson knew he needed to go to Barker Ranch, deeper into the desert, to avoid the worst of the anticipated uprisings. And that meant he had to spur Family members to work harder than they ever had.

"We never had newspapers at the Spahn Ranch, but Charlie got an *LA Times* with headlines about the Tate/LaBianca killings," Catherine Share later shared.

"He held it up and said, 'It's started.' He said we had to get out of town, because it was now dangerous. We were up day and night putting food into barrels and getting our last clothes together, the leather outfits we'd been working on. We had three dune buggies with roll bars and machine gun mounts. It was apocalyptic.

"No one spoke of any alternative."

Despite Manson's prohibition against eating meat, the Family did use furs and hides, both for its cars and its clothing. Since they would not kill animals, they had to buy or steal their skins.

They didn't give much thought to the inconsistency. They probably thought that animals were blameless, unlike people. But the reasons did not matter. Manson was, after all, their infallible leader. He also, of course, was insane.

Even so, he was still functioning—and at a high and dangerous level. He had warped the minds of Family members so thoroughly that they would prepare for carnage without thought of their former actual families or loved ones. He had instilled in them his messianic fervor.

"[W]e'd learn to live off the land," Share recalled. "We'd live in the desert and come in on dune buggies and rescue the orphaned white babies. We'd be the saviors.

"I believed that the cities were going to burn. I believed my only safety was to stay with the Family.

"I believed Charlie knew best."

Manson continued to prep the Barker Ranch for the Family's arrival. The ranch, which consisted of a series of stucco and stone buildings, was once pretty. It certainly had a gorgeous vista: it sat on a hill overlooking Death Valley.

And, of course, a settlement atop a hill is easier to defend.

In mid-August, he sent Tex Watson and Dianne Lake to the ranch. Watson was an obvious choice to be sent from Spahn, as he'd been involved with both the Tate and LaBianca murders. If anyone could be linked to both crimes, it would either be him or Patricia Krenwinkel.

Lake, at age fifteen, represented another liability for Manson. She was far and away the youngest non-baby member of the Family, and if she were around when any law enforcement agents happened to drop in, there would be a lot of questions

Manson would not want to answer. So she was sent to the relative isolation of Barker Ranch.

There was someone else Manson would have benefitted from sending away, but did not. Straight Satans treasurer Danny DeCarlo was still hanging around, keeping the weapons working, having sex whenever he felt like it, lying in the sun and drinking—despite Manson's low tolerance for alcohol, which he considered inefficient as a drug that allowed him to exert control. Manson continued to tolerate him because he was hoping to lure more of the Straight Satans onto the ranch to serve as a militia.

The irony of the messiah served by agents of "Satan" probably did not even occur to him.

Most of the other Straight Satans, however, were not interested in the Manson-centered religious offerings served up at Spahn Ranch. They were outlaws, not disciples. If they had to have a God, it was not going to be Charles Manson but Harley-Davidson.

Furthermore, the club wanted their treasurer back. On August 15, a double handful roared into Spahn Ranch, demanding that Manson turn DeCarlo over to them.

Manson greeted them with open arms. Some of the girls opened other limbs for them, simultaneously taking the edge off the bikers' fury and also splitting—and exhausting—the group. Once the motorcyclists' war fires had been cooled, they reconvened in the center of the movie sets that made up the ranch.

Manson had a surprise for them: DeCarlo was nowhere to be found. Neither were several rifles usually kept in the Family's gun racks. Manson's men were, in fact, on the roofs of the movie set. From atop the Longhorn Saloon, the Rock City Café, and other structures, Family members were armed and ready to pick off any Straight Satan who made a move on Manson. It was a trap straight out of the westerns filmed on the ranch. If there were any life into which reality and fantasy were destined to become a messy blur, it was that of Charlie Manson.

The Straight Satans backed down. They had no choice. But they left one of their own, Robert Reinhard, to find DeCarlo and convince him to return to them. To avoid having their trip seem like a total rout, they took back the cutlass Manson had been carrying ever since he snatched it from DeCarlo.

Within twenty-four hours, whatever plans the Straight Satans and the Family had had taken a sharp left turn. At dawn on Saturday, August 16, more than one hundred law-enforcement officials swarmed over the ranch, rousting sleepers, scaring animals, and seizing weapons and vehicles.

As helicopters buzzed overhead, ranch hands and Family members alike were rounded up like herds of cattle. In all, twenty-six people were arrested, including DeCarlo, Manson, and Reinhard. Over protests, a handful of babies and toddlers, including Linda Kasabian's daughter and DeCarlo's one-and-a-half-year-old son, were placed into foster homes.

Manson was dragged out from under one of the buildings and cuffed; he must have been terrified the raid was in response to the Tate and LaBianca killings. He was a messiah, but he was not prepared to be a martyr. When the arrest warrant indicated authorities were looking for automobiles, auto parts, and guns, it must have been a relief.

Manson would have been even more relieved when, two days later, all charges again him and his Family were dropped. The search warrant had the wrong date on it—the raid was originally scheduled three days earlier than it had occurred—and every one of the arrests was invalid. And with that, the Family returned to Spahn Ranch.

Unfortunately, the vehicles the Family had stolen, including all the cars that were being transformed into dune buggies, were not.

However, with the arrest—and the removal of the vehicles—at least one of Manson's problems was resolved. Most of the reasons DeCarlo would have had for staying were gone. Absent the promise of the motorcycle gang serving as a brute squad, and given DeCarlo's flouting of Manson's alcohol rules and not buying into Manson's philosophy, DeCarlo had little to offer the Family. So they stopped offering him anything he wanted. DeCarlo had no more reason to stay, and left the ranch within two weeks.

Goodbye, Donkey Dan. Goodbye, threat from the Straight Satans.

But not quite.

Without the lure of the Manson girls or the Spahn Ranch lifestyle, DeCarlo had no reason to keep Family secrets. After being picked up on unrelated charges a few months later, he traded evidence on the Manson Family for immunity.

While he was able to duck the local charges, DeCarlo did not get immunity on a federal gun charge. He opted to flee to Canada without collecting his share of the $25,000 reward Warren Beatty, Roman Polanski, and others had posted.

Manson, meanwhile, had a new concern. He could not figure out why the Spahn Ranch had been raided. The somewhat banal reason was that a police helicopter had seen a Volkswagen in a ditch on the ranch, checked its license plate, and determined that the car had been stolen. But Manson had no way of knowing that.

Lacking this knowledge, wondering if there might be spies or informants, paranoia within the Family was ratcheted to a new high. And it had a perfect target.

Donald "Shorty" Shea, who lived away from the ranch, had not been arrested. That was the same Shea whom Lynette Fromme had heard ranch owner George Spahn recommend be used as a spy against the Family. The same Shea who had beaten the crap out of Manson earlier in 1969.

On August 15, 1969, Shea delivered yet another affront to Manson.

Manson, who had preached fear of the militant black man.

Manson, whose path to glory was grounded in the idea that blacks were intellectually inferior and, post-Helter Skelter, would have no choice but to recognize his superiority and crown him their leader.

Manson, who was being targeted by the Black Panthers for having killed one of theirs, or so he thought.

On this day, Shea brought his new wife to the Spahn Ranch. He had met the woman Magdalena (sometimes Magdalene) three months previously. She had been performing in a topless bar in Carson, California that Shea managed. She was beautiful. She was bold.

She was black.

When they were introduced, Manson was incensed. As Manson processed the personal disrespect, let alone the clear security breach of introducing a black person to their hideout, he was filled with fury.

In essence, Shorty Shea was a dead man walking.

Shea was a big, tough man, and it was going to require several people to take him down . . . and not all of them were going to be in the inner circle.

Early one morning on August 26, a few weeks after the Tate/LaBianca killings, Manson pulled Bruce Davis, Clem Grogan, Bill Vance, and Tex Watson aside.

Shea was an informant, Manson said. He needed to die, and they would be the ones to take his life.

Davis would later be asked why he would readily kill someone for Manson with virtually no evidence against that person. Davis said his mental moral facilities had "declined over time," possibly as a result of his being distanced from society; possibly as a result of the ever-present drug supplies at the ranch. Physical isolation, control of the media, forging personal relationships, and the use of drugs are four of the cornerstones of mind control by cults and by nations. With intuitive sophistication, Manson had deployed them all.

"The state I was in . . . I didn't ask any questions," Davis replied.

Like so much of what went on within both the Family and Manson's corrupted head, there was probably more than one reason why Shea was killed. The *least* likely is that Manson felt Shea was a snitch. But he needed a reason that would resonate with anyone he asked to help him. And acting for the good of the Family, and Charlie Manson, had been set up as the most noble possible justification.

But there were a few other reasons. His wife was a big one. The beating he had given Manson earlier in the year was a wound that had continued to fester. His refusal to join the Family was a personal rejection. Each, in Manson's mind, was all the justification he would need.

At the start of the workday on August 26, the men approached Shea; they needed a lift to where the Family stored auto parts for the cars it repaired and the fresh supply of dune buggies it was building. Shea drove, which would divert his attention from the others in the vehicle. Tex Watson sat next to him in the passenger seat. Clem Grogan sat behind Shea, and Davis was behind Watson.

Manson followed in a second car. They never made it to the auto parts area.

During the ride, Watson told Shea to pull over. Shea refused, and Watson stabbed him. Message received. Shea parked near an embankment. From the backseat, Grogan smacked Shea's head with a pipe.

Still alive, still vaguely aware, Shea was pulled from behind the wheel and half-dragged, half-thrown down the embankment. Then, like human coyotes, Watson and Grogan set on him, stabbing and beating him.

Davis initially stayed behind in the car, but there was no way Manson would allow that. When Manson pulled up, he quietly went to Davis and quietly urged, "C'mon." And so Davis followed.

For this particular target, Manson was going to get his hands dirty, joining Grogan and Watson in stabbing Shea.

Davis had a machete, and Manson had wanted him to cut Shea's head off—but he couldn't as his knife was too blunt. Manson was not going to let him off without doing some damage, however, so Davis hacked at Shea's shoulder with a knife.

In his dying moments, Shea looked at Manson and pleaded, "Charlie, why are you doing this?"

"Here's why," Manson said, mustering fresh hate and stabbing him again.

Never ask why.

The four buried Shea and returned to the ranch. There were several factors that kept the murder of Donald Shea from being the perfect crime.

The biggest was that most of the people involved could not keep their mouths shut.

Once again, whispers started on the ranch, both internally and externally. Shorty had fled. Shorty was dead. Shorty had been cut up into nine parts, each of which was buried somewhere. Davis himself helped spread that rumor, boasting to Straight Satans member Alan Springer that they had cut off Shea's limbs and buried the parts around the ranch. The "nine parts" rumor persisted until Clem Grogan drew his map of where the body was buried in 1985, which would help secure his parole.

The next day, a few Family members gathered up Shea's belongings, threw them into his car, and abandoned it in the Los Angeles suburb of Canoga Park.

During the next few days, Family members casually mentioned around that Shea had gone to San Francisco to pursue a job opportunity.

* * *

The previous few weeks had delivered a few unexpected and unprecedented cracks in Manson's seeming omnipotence.

First, there was the raid. The Family was too cut off from society to know whether Helter Skelter was really starting—but if it had, it was not widespread enough to prevent law enforcement from sparing the manpower to converge on Spahn Ranch.

Donald Shea's disappearance would not normally have been a big deal—he supplemented his income from Spahn Ranch with all sorts of offsite jobs—but there had been rumors among the less plugged-in Family members that he had not really gone to San Francisco. Translation: Manson had lied to them.

And the dune buggies that were supposed to bring the Family from the admittedly unpleasant Barker Ranch to the bottomless pit were gone, although Manson had put a premium on raising cash and car thefts to replace them. How had their leader not foreseen something that big and had a backup plan?

Finally, the Family was under-equipped and everyone knew it. While they still had caches of guns and fuel that had been buried, it was much more difficult to hide dune buggies and other vehicles, and the authorities, aided by helicopters, had done a good job of rooting them from their hiding spots. The Family stole a few cars, perhaps taking risks it might not have under different circumstances. But there was no time to be cautious, if they ever were. The Family, minus a few women left behind so the welcome mat at Spahn Ranch would not be completely rolled up but plus a handful of newer recruits, was going to go deep into the desert of Death Valley.

To a large degree, the return of familiar routine re-established both Manson's control and a sense of general well-being among the Family.

By the end of the first week in September, most of the Family had resettled at Barker Ranch. Manson kept them busy preparing for an attack, although who exactly was going to attack them—the Black Panthers, the Straight Satans, another round of law enforcement—changed as frequently as Manson's mood.

Men were assigned guard duty, which kept them isolated, in the shade, and off the harsher work details. Manson instinctively knew what political leaders since the Roman emperor Octavius have known: above all, keep your military happy.

Manson's girls were kept busy cooking, cleaning, and chopping firewood in the desert heat. For them, a cushy work detail—one in which men participated as well—was grabbing one of the dune buggies and going into the desert, looking for the bottomless pit Manson promised would lead them to an underground paradise, where they would wait out Helter Skelter.

The desert lectures continued, but the free-love idyll of *Stranger in a Strange Land* was gone. This was the trial by fire; Manson's nightly sermons, augmented by acid whenever he could get it, were now almost exclusively about the next world. It was one of the few enticements he could still offer. Food supplies were low, reflecting the Family's isolation. Drugs, so useful in keeping his followers docile, were available only sporadically. But the promise of a world to come was something he could draw on without limits.

"He felt a weird sense of responsibility when the Family thing was happening and they were in the desert," said Marlin Marynick. "I think when he hit a point where he thought The Beatles were talking to him and there's going to be this race war and they have to dig into the center of the earth . . . to me it sounds like a psychotic break. I think the guy had a nervous breakdown," he added. He had experience with this type of thing from his time working as a psychiatric nurse. "Everyone calls him a master manipulator. I don't see it, myself—I think they were all fending for themselves, but there was a lot of drugs, a lot of communal living and I think he obviously had some mental health issues for sure."

Some seemed to buy into the religious mania wholeheartedly. Leslie Van Houten was not shy about describing herself in divine terms.

"I think I'm an angel, so to speak," she would later tell one of her attorneys.

"Not with wings, you know. Naturally I know I don't have wings. But . . . I believe I'm one of the disciples. I'm one of the people spoken about in the Bible."

Was Van Houten angling for a diminished capacity consideration when she said that? It's possible, but believing that flies in the face of the effective brainwashing techniques Manson had used on his group.

Furthermore, Van Houten was only one among many who, whether through desire to believe Manson or sheer exhaustion, had surrendered to his vision.

And Manson's visions *were* getting wilder. Like a prophet in the wilderness, isolation affected him, too. Paul Watkins described how Manson painted a vivid picture of the bottomless pit the Family was seeking.

The entrance would be guarded by rattlesnakes, and the Family's first lesson would be making friends with the snakes and learning how to get around them, according to Watkins. In his prison writings posted online, he also described how once past the snakes, there would be a series of chambers and tunnels which would eventually open into a city of gold.

There would be light without sun. And, in an image taken from Revelation 22:2, there would be trees that bore fruit, with a single tree producing a different type of delicious fruit every month.

To people scrabbling in the hard soil of the desert, that alone would have sounded like paradise.

But Manson was not the only one talking. While he did his best to keep the Family constantly occupied, if not in a state of perpetual exhaustion, the isolation of the Barker and Myers ranches loosened tongues.

"In early September, I was taking a nap in the bedroom at Myers Ranch, a half mile away" from Barker Ranch, Barbara Hoyt later recalled.

"I woke up and heard Sadie [Susan Atkins] talking to Ruth Ann Morehouse. I didn't pay any attention until I heard the name 'Tate.' Then I started listening. She said that Sharon Tate was the last to die, that she had to watch the others die first. She said that Sharon had called for her mother. She said that Abigail had called for God, and she said that Tex ran over and gutted her."

These were the people with whom Hoyt was living in isolation. She was hours away from the nearest settlement, which was over desert terrain. But by early October, she did not care. She grabbed Sherry Cooper—one of the other Manson girls she felt she could trust—and the two of them walked through desert terrain to Ballarat, a former supply point for mining operations.

Cooper was a good choice for Hoyt's traveling companion. She had been involved with Danny DeCarlo, and apparently shared his concerns about the Family.

But before that could happen, the girls had to get to safety. The town of Ballarat lies just under 22 miles north and west of Barker Ranch, and Family members who had been living at Barker would occasionally go to its general store for supplies.

Hoyt would later estimate it took them between fifteen and sixteen hours to walk there. This may have been because they were moving slowly due to heat or exhaustion. Or they may have been careful to stay hidden in what little cover they could find when they heard anyone coming; Manson had posted armed guards around the perimeter of the ranch, nominally to keep trespassers out.

Or, given Manson's refusal to let them have watches, they may have just overestimated their journey.

Regardless, it must have been grueling, and there was not much there for the girls when they arrived. At its peak, Ballarat had three hotels, seven saloons, and a post office, but its peak had been right around 1900. By the time Cooper and Hoyt showed up, it had little more than the general store. Still, one of the four or five people who lived there gave the girls a lift to Los Angeles.

After Cooper fled Barker Ranch, she and DeCarlo would go to Canada together and get married.

Hoyt stayed with her family—her biological family, alternating between her grandmother's and mother's homes. But during the first months away from Manson, she remained certain the Family would come for her.

"I slept all day and stayed up all night," she would later tell *Los Angeles* magazine. "I kept my mother's biggest kitchen knife with me. I was guarding the house. I went from one window to another."

"When I told my mother what I knew, she didn't want to believe it."

Cooper and Hoyt were not the only people at Barker Ranch who had seen flaws in their leader. Spahn Ranch worker Juan Flynn did not consider himself a Family member, but had gone into the desert with Manson in an attempt to pick up clues about what had happened to Donald Shea. By this point, Manson and others were openly bragging about what they had done.

That knowledge did not do Flynn much good. The Family had only a few vehicles, so taking one and trying to bolt would have caused suspicion. Besides, there were the armed guards Manson had posted—the same ones Cooper and Hoyt had avoided by quietly walking away from the ranch. Juan waited, looking for an opportunity to do . . . something.

Manson would ultimately give Flynn his opportunity. By early September 1969, when the Family began using the ranch as its primary base, Brooks Poston and Paul Watkins were occasionally seen prospecting with Paul Crockett, the miner who had pulled them from the Family.

In mid-September, Manson approached Crockett, trying to draw the prospector and his two former Family assistants back into the fold, but Crockett stood his ground.

Manson had another reason for engaging Crockett: The prospector had managed to pull two of his Family members from him.

"[H]e knew he had the power to get people to do anything he wanted once he got them," Crockett said. "What he was more interested in was, how did I . . . undo what he had already done to them?"

Crockett was willing to engage in discussions about Scientology with Manson, but he was not going to give too much away about how he had been able to lure away Manson's followers. As long as Crockett kept a little mystery, he maintained his chances of staying alive.

Crockett was also willing, on a very limited basis, to help Manson transport supplies to Barker Ranch. It was all part of being a good, cooperative neighbor. *Your people can work with me. We can help each other.*

And again, being useful helped keep him off Manson's hit list . . . or so he thought.

Having failed to co-opt Crockett, Manson turned to his fallback solution—eliminating him. But again, Manson made a poor choice. Rather than turn to one in his inner circle to do the job, he decided to entrust Juan Flynn with the task.

Flynn was tall, physically imposing, strong from all the ranch work he had done, and a Vietnam vet. He was a perfect choice to serve as Manson's hit man.

Except it didn't work. Like Poston and Watkins before him, Flynn threw his lot in with the prospector. Manson was incensed.

Fate once again threw an obstacle in the way of Manson getting revenge on Crockett. This time, the obstacle was physical. The Family had been tearing up the desert in a variety of vehicles, including dune buggies, a Ford rented with a stolen credit card and a four-wheel-drive red Toyota Land Cruiser stolen shortly before the move to Barker Ranch. On September 19, Family members came across a Michigan front-end loader earth-moving machine blocking one of their favorite roads.

Manson ordered it set on fire. Speculation regarding why has ranged from his fury at the road being blocked—yet another challenge to his authority—to what the machine represented in terms of environmental damage. This impulse turned out as well as Manson's other crimes. Inyo County had just paid $35,000—close to a quarter million dollars at 2019 prices—for the machine. County officials wanted heads.

Park rangers investigated. They noted several sets of tire tracks leading from the crime scene, including those belonging to a Toyota Land Cruiser. When they asked around the few people within driving distance of the incident, they heard that yes, people had seen a Land Cruiser recently. A bright red one, which was being driven by some hippies who lived up around the Barker Ranch.

On September 29, Powell and California Highway Patrolman James Pursell visited Barker Ranch, but did not find much. Only two of the Manson girls were in residence, with the rest of the Family having gone out on various errands. They had also taken their vehicles with them.

Bad luck. But the rangers got some good luck as they were driving away when they came across a truck containing two prospectors. Brooks Poston was at the wheel, and next to him was Paul Crockett.

The two seemed nervous, and after interviewing them police understood why. They told a wild tale of a messianic hippie cult in which sex, drugs, and preparing for a racial war were the orders of the day. They also were storing tires, tanks of gasoline, and weapons in stashes throughout the desert.

Intrigued, Powell and Pursell turned around and did a sweep of the area around Barker Ranch. This time, they ran into seven of the Manson girls, camped out and enjoying the sun. Several were enjoying it fully—they were completely naked.

Lynette Fromme, who had been sunbathing in the altogether, stood up as the officers approached. Pursell demanded to know who they were and what they were doing, but could not help noticing she was a natural redhead.

"We're a Girl Scout troop from the Bay Area," Fromme said. "Would you and the ranger like to be our scoutmasters?"

They clearly were *not* Girl Scouts. Girl Scouts would not have had two vehicles, each with gun scabbards holding a rifle, near their campsite. One was a dune buggy.

The other was a red four-wheel-drive Land Cruiser.

Pursell took the vehicle identification numbers from each car. He could not call them in, as his radio would not work in the valley. But when Pursell returned to his station, he ran them. Unsurprisingly, both came back listed as stolen.

* * *

Crockett and Poston were spooked; the Family had been creepy crawling around their lodgings.

"[T]his Charlie . . . he can sneak into your camp, he can sit six feet from you in the back of a window or something like that and hear everything that is going on. The next time he sees you he tells you your whole conversation, and he starts laughing," Crockett would tell investigators.

During the next few days, Crockett and Poston would end up speaking to more park rangers, sheriffs, and highway patrolmen, filling out the picture at Barker Ranch. They were advised to leave the site immediately.

Manson knew Crockett was speaking to law enforcement, and paid him one final visit.

"He said I should be more afraid of him than I was of the law," Crockett said. "And he said it with a straight face, calmly and everything else. And that is the first time he had ever put on a straight face with me."

Crockett and Poston went back to their base and packed while Flynn was out scouting for alternate locations where the prospectors could live and work; Paul Watkins had been shuttling back and forth between Barker Ranch and Crockett's site.

Crockett and Poston packed a few cans of food and walked 20 miles through the desert. They would eventually rendezvous with Flynn and Watkins at a new site in the appropriately named Independence, California.

* * *

Tex Watson, too, was having doubts as the Family lived at the Barker Ranch. The heat was oppressive and the drug supply was thin. In addition, Manson had been more prone to anger. The endless hours of guard duty were not as much fun as the time spent doing auto repair, or playing music, or being able to have sex with whomever he wanted.

Then Powell and Pursell started sniffing around Barker Ranch.

Manson felt sure they would soon come back. He gave Watson a shotgun and told him to kill them. With that, Charlie Manson, leader of the Family, savior and messiah who would lead his followers into the glories of the bottomless pit as they sang songs he wrote, left the ranch on a fundraising run.

For Watson, being ordered to murder law enforcement was finally going too far. "[T]he next morning I took off in an old pickup and ran from Charlie. I drove the truck as far as it would go. I hitchhiked to the city, called my parents for money, and flew to Texas."

There is a key difference between paranoia and fear. Fear arises from a clear and present threat. With paranoia, someone *suspects* that enemy forces are out to get them. A grandiose person can believe he is smarter, stronger, or otherwise better equipped to fend those forces off.

Manson had been paranoid for a while. But with the loss of Watson, fear came to the forefront. Tex had been involved in eight Family killings—including Donald Shea's, in which Manson, too, had an active hand. Losing Watson—losing *control* of Watson—made Manson vulnerable to being prosecuted, if he were again arrested.

Manson could not have known that Watson, back in his home state, would spend several weeks in a near-catatonic state. He had had—or really wanted people to think he had—a complete mental breakdown.

Manson likely would not have cared. During his sermons, when he would draw on his prison experiences, he always said that if he were arrested, he would "act crazy" in prison to avoid being hassled. If Family members ever heard of him being crazy while locked up, they would do well to remember that was just Charlie once again outplaying the system.

There was no reason to believe Watson would not do the same. After all, Manson had taught him well.

With Watson gone, Manson was running out of males he could rely on. The only one left was Clem Grogan. So when Manson left, the Family's enforcement branch was being headed by a young man people called Scramblehead. Kathy Lutesinger, well into her second trimester with Bobby Beausoleil's child, saw a chance. On the night of October 9, 1969, she tapped Manson's main squeeze,

Stephanie Schram. That night, the two set out from Barker Ranch. Yet again, they proved Manson girls should not be confused with Girl Scouts. Absent a compass or knowledge of navigation by starlight, they walked a wide circle around the ranch, rather than away from it.

Dawn was coming. With it, their absence would be discovered. And then Grogan, who was eager to prove he would kill for Charlie Manson, who had access to several dune buggies, would be after them.

Although they did not know it, however, the cavalry was coming.

Shortly before dawn on October 10, a small joint force made up of officers from the California Highway Patrol, Inyo County Sheriff's Department, and the National Parks Service maneuvered into position around Barker Ranch. Some were on foot, as the terrain would not allow most vehicles to pass—especially being that Family members had piled rocks in the roads.

One team, which was approaching the ranch from the west, was riding in on a Toyota Land Cruiser owned by one of the officers. It was one of the few vehicles the force had that could travel across the rough terrain.

The first Family members picked up were, perhaps, payback for Manson's misplaced faith. On a hilltop, supposedly on guard duty but actually fast asleep with a sawed-off shotgun between them, were two guards. One was fifteen-year-old Hugh "Rocky" Todd, a relatively new recruit. The other was Manson's handpicked consigliere, Clem Grogan. The team in the Land Cruiser found and arrested them. Another lookout, eighteen-year-old Robert Ivan Lane, was also apprehended by that team.

There had been three arrests without even one shot being fired.

James Pursell, the California Highway Patrol officer who had gone to Barker Ranch two weeks before, and his partners, officers Jack O'Neil and Dave Steiber, were part of a team approaching from the east. O'Neil spotted a small cave, somewhat protected from the elements by sheets of corrugated steel covered in dirt and sagebrush, in the side of a rise. O'Neil decided to hike around the rise so he could approach the cave from above. Pursell and Steiber remained in place, keeping an eye on it.

As the sun rose, they watched as three girls—Patricia Krenwinkel, Catherine Share, and Leslie Van Houten—ambled out of the cave and leisurely stretched.

When they were done, they went back into the cave. The girls never saw Pursell and Steiber.

The two officers crept toward the cave. When they were close, O'Neil picked up a large rock and dropped it on the corrugated steel. The noise was sharp in the gully. To those in the cave, it must have been deafening. They would later complain about having been shot at.

"Come on out of there!" ordered O'Neil.

The three girls did.

When the officers went into the cave, they found military field phones, the sort that are operated by a crank. They would find another one in the main cabin. The cave was being set up as a lookout point, but it had not been finished. It never would be.

No phone line meant the girls in the cave could not call the ranch house (while east and west teams approached the ranch house together). In short order they arrested Susan Atkins, twenty-three-year-old Madaline Cottage, and Lynette Fromme.

After the girls were placed in custody, Pursell did a quick head count. Where were the three guards who had been arrested?

Lane had been captured near a site called the Lotus Mine. The officers glimpsed him when he popped his head up from behind a rock. They had nabbed him and handcuffed him to an inch-and-a-half water pipe that led into the mine.

And Grogan and Todd?

"There was a big ore car beside the road, and [arresting officer Ben Anderson] said they handcuffed them around its axle and told them if they could carry that ore car then they were free to go," Pursell said.

As the Barker Ranch teams started to pack up, two more girls came running out from an encampment.

It was Kathy Lutesinger and Stephanie Schram, who flagged the officers down and gave themselves up.

At the nearby Myers Ranch, another raiding party effortlessly rounded up Sandra Good, Ruth Ann Moorehouse, Nancy Pitman, and Diane Von Ahn, whose age was variously given as nineteen or twenty-one.

The raids had netted three men, ten girls, and two babies—Susan Atkins's son

Zezozose, and Sunstone Hawk, whom Good had given birth to a month before. Both were sunburned and malnourished. They were immediately put under the care of a matron.

The raid turned up dune buggies, most of which had been made from stolen cars; a pistol; several knives; food; gasoline; and other survivalist supplies. The teams also found sleeping bags—more than the thirteen needed for those just arrested, indicating there were people living at the ranch who had not been caught. The raiding party would need to return for the rest.

All thirteen were brought to a jail in Independence, California. Steiber began interrogating the two girls who had given themselves up. He also called their homes. One of the parents told him their daughter was being sought by the Los Angeles County Sheriff's Department as a witness to a homicide. Steiber reached out to the department.

"He got a hold of a detective down there, and the detective said, 'Hold. On. To. Them,'" Pursell recalled.

In the pre-cable days of 1969, the town of Independence did not get a lot of television news, and the only newspaper regularly serving the community was published in San Bernardino. Officers there had not received a lot of information about the Tate/LaBianca killings, and certainly would not have known about Gary Hinman or Donald Shea.

Pursell made good on his plan to go back to two days later. On October 12, he and three park rangers headed toward Barker Ranch. Along the way, they passed a stake bed truck loaded with drums of gasoline, dried food, and boxes of cold-weather gear that had gotten stuck in the sand.

Manson had scored on his cash run, and was bringing back a bounty.

Pursell called for backup, and he and his team continued toward Barker Ranch.

Two rangers set themselves up so they could cover both the front and side doors to the main cabin. Pursell and another ranger went to a vantage point and waited. Soon enough, they saw four people walking toward the cabin, including one bearded man clad head to toe in buckskin, to whom the others were clearly deferring. None of them saw the rangers as they entered the cabin.

The sun was setting, and Pursell did not want to start a gunfight at night.

When he saw reinforcements from the sheriff's department in the distance, he decided to act.

Pursell and the rangers moved in, two to a door. Pursell drew his gun and threw open his door. Several Family members were sitting around a table, and Pursell told them to put their hands on their heads.

"And . . . everyone ignored me," Pursell said. "I thought, 'This isn't how it's done in the movies.'"

He repeated his order, emphasizing it with his gun. This time, they all obeyed. The rangers led them out of the cabin, one by one. Very soon, Family members including Bruce Davis, John Philip Haught, and Dianne Lake were all under arrest.

Charlie Manson was nowhere to be found.

It was getting dark, and the cabin was not wired for electricity. There was a candle in a glass mug on the dining room table, which Pursell grabbed with his left hand. Leading with his right—his gun hand—he went into the small bathroom.

The flickering candle revealed a sink with a small cupboard beneath it. The door to the cupboard was slightly open, and strands of long chestnut-colored hair were sticking out.

Pursell stood still, holding the candle and pointing his gun at the cupboard, which slowly opened further.

"[T]his figure starts unwinding and coming out," Pursell said. "How he got into that cupboard, I'll never know."

"Hi!" said Charlie Manson.

"Make one wrong move and I'll blow your head off," replied Pursell.

Through the years, people have asked Pursell what stopped him from just shooting Manson at that moment.

"We really didn't know what we had," Pursell explains. "And you can't just shoot someone that climbs out of a little cupboard and says, 'Hi!'"

Pursell led Manson to where the others were waiting, and went back to check the last room.

Manson Family member Bill Vance was standing in the doorway to the bedroom.

"I then realized I had my back to him the entire time I was pulling Charlie out,"

Pursell said. "But as we learned later, nobody would do anything without the order from Charlie."

During the drive to jail, Manson made one request. When he and the three other men had hiked to the cabin, he had stashed his guitar behind a rock to lighten his load. Might he be permitted to get off the truck and retrieve it?

Request denied. We can never know what was behind the query, whether he might have been looking for a desperate effort to escape or seeking a totem to get him through the ordeal ahead.

The Family members were charged with grand theft auto, arson—stemming from the burning of the earth mover—and a variety of other charges. The buckskin-clad leader of the group was booked as Manson, Charles M., a.k.a. Jesus Christ, God. If there were a way the madman could possibly have been angry and pleased at the same time, that was it.

Authorities retrieved eleven vehicles during the raids. While most were stolen, there was no way of linking which of the people arrested were involved in their theft. After a few days, more than half were released, including Bruce Davis, Squeaky Fromme, Sandy Good, and Christopher Haught. They began drifting back to Los Angeles, with some winding up back at Spahn Ranch. Fromme and Good rented a motel room near the jail so they could serve those still in custody.

Those in jail were resolutely loyal to Manson. They had to believe, in their hearts, that he would somehow get them out of this to continue the journey.

Other Family members, however, were talking.

Kitty Lutesinger, who had been picked up during the Barker Ranch raid, was working with investigators and trying to spread the blame. After all, her boyfriend Bobby Beausoleil was being held for the murder of Gary Hinman.

She told investigators he had gone with two other women to collect money from Hinman. Unfortunately, she could only remember the name of one who had been bragging: Susan Atkins.

Manson himself did not seem to have done much in the way of killings, but Lutesinger recalled seeing him at the wheel of one of the stolen dune buggies. Though not enough to pin a grand theft auto rap on him, it would keep him in jail a little while longer.

Lutesinger's allegations were enough to get Atkins transferred to the Sybil Brand

Institute, a Los Angeles County jail for female inmates. Murder suspicions would trump car theft and arson suspicions, especially because it was hard to tie any specific individual arrested at the Barker or Myers ranches to a given stolen automobile or burning the earth mover. All of the charges would eventually be dropped.

Atkins initially believed her transfer reflected Beausoleil giving her up as part of his defense. But as she participated in the preliminary hearings for his trial, she realized Lutesinger was helping the prosecution. And with her transfer, she was no longer in Manson's orbit. She would have to rely on her own wits to protect herself.

Even without her drugged and psychologically damaged brain, she would have been extremely hard-pressed to do that.

The move also placed her among a rougher crowd than the then-twenty-one-year-old had been used to. She adapted by taking Manson's advice to act crazy when in jail, although for her it may have come more naturally. She put on an intense persona, giggling inappropriately, twirling randomly, and singing little songs—often Manson's, of course.

She got chummy with her bunkmates, thirty-seven-year-old self-described party girl Virginia Graham, who had violated her parole, and thirty-three-year-old Ronnie Howard, who was in for forging a prescription. The two older women had been petty criminals for a good chunk of their adult lives, and Atkins felt the need to run with, if not surpass, them.

Initially, Graham and Howard dismissed her boasts as those of a little girl seeking attention. The wild stories about this Charlie she was following, a mystic religious leader who was going to lead the blacks after a race war, were beyond fantastic. But Atkins persisted, and she also displayed a fair amount of detailed knowledge about the murders.

At first, Atkins limited herself to talking about the Hinman murder. But she was with Graham and Howard 24 hours a day, and could only get so much shock value out of the same story. Slowly, details from the Tate killings crept into her tales.

Atkins likely thought nothing of her boasts. She had done so when she was alone with the Family and not gotten into trouble, and here in prison she was building a new family.

Graham and Howard thought differently. In time, they came to wonder whether this manic girl might be telling at least something of the truth. Prison rules about snitching are close to universal, but there was a difference between boasting about past crimes and revealing the intent to do more. And Atkins was claiming that, in order to start the race war she kept calling Helter Skelter, there would be more killings.

* * *

Back at the Sybil Brand Institute, Howard begged a guard to let her call the Los Angeles police, or at least to make a call on her behalf.

The guard said that she was not authorized to do so.

Howard would not have a chance to make a phone call to investigators until mid-November, just shy of a month after Atkins had started talking to her. But by the end of November, she was able to talk; the ties between the Family and the Tate/LaBianca killings were forming. Furthermore, the teams investigating the killings, which had been separate, were sharing information.

Prisoners and Family members were not the only ones with something to say. On the outside, the outlaws were talking to the cops.

Danny DeCarlo of the Straight Satans had been picked up on a few minor charges which, given his record, could have resulted in solid jail time. But he had something to trade. He'd been hanging with a group of hippies for a while, and had heard a few things about some serious crimes, especially those that had been in the news in August. Were the cops interested? DeCarlo gave up a lot of second-hand information about the Hinman, Tate, and LaBianca killings, including the fact that Charlie Manson had used a cutlass he stole from DeCarlo to slash Hinman's face. That cutlass was now back in the possession of the Straight Satans.

There was more physical evidence DeCarlo could offer. There had been guns, or at least a gun, used in the Tate and Hinman killings. DeCarlo did not have the gun, but he did know where, on the Spahn Ranch, the Family took target practice. Might be some interesting ballistic evidence there.

There was just one problem. As Family members were released from the Barker Ranch raid, they had drifted back to Spahn. DeCarlo was happy to play tour guide, but he asked to be put in handcuffs so it would not look as though he had a choice in cooperating.

Nobody likes a snitch.

The search was done with George Spahn's permission, so the investigators were spared the trouble of getting a warrant. At the ranch, they found slugs and shell casings . . . but no gun.

In his cell in the Independence jail, Manson was mulling what the strengths and weaknesses of the case against him might be. The car raps he could beat— after all, he had done so before.

But the murders . . . Manson had been losing control of those who had been involved with them. It did not console him to imagine that, after all, so had Jesus. Because Manson did not want his story to end the same way.

He worried about Atkins . . . she who was so wild and unpredictable that he would periodically send her away when important people were around. Atkins who, more than any other girl, would challenge him for the spotlight. Atkins who was now many miles from him. She could be a problem . . . and he knew it.

The little girls who had run away from him, Cooper, Hoyt, Lutesinger, and Schram, along with anyone else who might have drifted away after the Barker Ranch raids, angered him, but they were not part of the inner circle.

Clem Grogan still loved him, and at any rate Grogan was locked up alongside him. Bruce Davis, Manson was pretty sure, would remain quiet.

There was, however, one relative newcomer who might be a problem.

John Philip "Zero" Haught had joined the Family some time before the October 12, 1969, raid on Barker Ranch. By now he and a few other Family members moved into a house rented by Mark Ross, who had hung around the Family in 1968. Haught had earned a reputation for being a talker. He could not be trusted to put Charlie above himself, and that sealed his fate.

On November 5, 1969, Haught was at Ross's home with four other Family members. One later told investigators she and Haught had been in bed when he decided to play Russian roulette with a .22 Caliber Iver Johnson revolver. Haught assured Cottage there was only one bullet in the gun, spun the cylinder, aimed the barrel at his head, and pulled the trigger.

The gun had been fully loaded. Both it, and its holster, had been wiped clean of fingerprints.

Investigators did not realize the four people in the home were Manson Family members. If they had, they might have been more inclined to treat the case as a murder, as opposed to a stoned hippie accidentally offing himself.

Chances are, it was Manson-ordered—or, more in keeping with his style, Manson-suggested—that Haught was a liability who needed to be neutralized. Despite being in jail, Manson was being attended to by Fromme and Good, and had ample communication opportunities with the remaining Family members.

At least one of Manson's followers was shaken by news of Haught's death. On November 26, 1969, after Leslie Van Houten has been transferred to the Sybil Brand Institute, she was interviewed by Los Angeles Police Department Sergeant Michael J. McGann. The interview contained the following exchange:

> **Van Houten:** [H]earing about Zero [Haught] has sort of thrown me for a loop because I know—I knew Zero and I know that Zero wouldn't play Russian roulette.
>
> **McGann:** That's what I think, too.
>
> **Van Houten:** Well, I know that—that Zero wouldn't because I saw him the day he got released [after the Barker Ranch raid]. I've never seen a happier person.
>
> **McGann:** It's officially listed as a suicide.
>
> **Van Houten:** I'm sure. But I—I really don't know. I don't know who would be doing that.
>
> . . .
>
> **Van Houten:** Zero was playing Russian roulette all by himself?
>
> **McGann:** Kind of odd, isn't it?

Haught's death was not investigated further and nobody was ever charged.

* * *

On November 26, Bobby Beausoleil's murder trial ended in a hung jury, which was good news for Manson. Beausoleil had gone through the entire process without, apparently, bringing up Manson's name. He was crossed off as a concern, even if he was going to be re-tried.

Tex Watson, unfortunately, had turned up, thanks to cooperation from Lutesinger. Watson had been arrested in Texas, but the state was fighting extradition to California. He would ultimately be brought to California in late 1970, and tried separately from Manson.

On December 1, police located and arrested Patricia Krenwinkel in Alabama. Spurred by the testimony of Virginia Graham and Ronnie Howard, Los Angeles Police Chief Edward Davis held a news conference in which he named three people for whom warrants had been issued: Linda Kasabian, who had yet to be found; Krenwinkel, who was freshly in custody; and Charlie Manson. More names would be shortly forthcoming, Davis added.

The most important aspect, Davis said, was that the case had been cracked.

It had, but it was weak and largely built around Atkins's testimony. Given her role in the Hinman, Tate, and LaBianca murders, along with her seeming pride in her role, prosecuting attorney Vincent Bugliosi was reluctant to offer any sort of deal. But Davis had been feeling pressure to show progress in a high-profile case, and needed to offer meat to the media.

As it would turn out, Davis's gamble would work to the prosecution's benefit. The media now had a name, and free from the rigors of police-style investigative work, was able to start slapping together stories about Manson and his band of hippies that ranged from factual to fantastic. Sketches, and then photographs, of the Family's captivating leader began to circulate.

Then, on December 4, Richard Caballero, Susan Atkins's defense attorney, inked a deal designed to save her from the gas chamber. In return for honest and complete grand jury testimony, the prosecution would not seek the death penalty. Prosecutor Vincent Bugliosi, who saw her as the craziest and most dangerous of the participants, was incensed at the offer. But the District Attorney's office was convinced her testimony was necessary for murder indictments against the other participants.

* * *

Atkins's grand jury testimony, which she gave on December 5, 1969, has shaped descriptions of the Tate murders for half a century. It was vivid and compelling. It was also, at times, heartless. Buoyed by the promise of immunity from whatever she said, Atkins described her role in the killings with relish. Next, Bugliosi showed her the photo of Steven Parent's body sprawled in the driver's seat of his car, the front of his short-sleeved plaid shirt awash with his blood after Watson had shot him four times.

Bugliosi asked Atkins to identify it.

Atkins: That is the thing I saw in the car.
Bugliosi: When you say "thing," you are referring to a human being?
Atkins: Yes, human being.

When members of the grand jury began to realize what they were hearing, they paled. The jury foreman had to call for several breaks during her testimony. While others would be called during the two days the grand jury was convened, hers would have been enough.

As Bugliosi would later describe, several of the people in the grand jury were sickened by her testimony.

Atkins also spoke of her love for Charlie Manson. Blind fealty is not a crime. The only question would be whether prosecutors could turn her words into his guilt for the murders he did not physically do.

It was certainly enough to return indictments. On Monday, December 8, 1969, Atkins, Linda Kasabian, Patricia Krenwinkel, Charles Manson, and Tex Watson were charged with seven counts of murder and one count of conspiracy to commit murder. Van Houten, who had only been along on the LaBianca killings, was charged with two counts of murder and one count of conspiracy to commit murder.

The prosecutors were not the only ones nervous about Atkins's professed obedience of Manson. Defense attorney Caballero was concerned she might recant her testimony once the actual trial started and she was facing the object of her devotion. He quietly arranged for the interviews she had done with his office to be turned into a quickie book.

A gag order had been imposed on the court, and Atkins's story was only supposed to be published in Europe. Of course, that seal crumbled—the *Los Angeles Times* got hold of a copy and reprinted it.

Anyone who bought a newspaper now knew exactly what the prosecution's star witness was going to claim. And that included Charlie Manson, who was getting ready to serve as his own attorney.

Manson had one other piece of very important information. If the report in the newspaper could be trusted, Atkins still thought Manson was a messiah.

* * *

The counterculture, anti-establishment revolution had been given an evil, wild-eyed face. But unlike modern crime tales, which draw upon forensic analysis, DNA and advanced policing techniques, this one had significant gaps.

Atkins's details resulted in people filling in some of the holes of the crime. She described in general terms where the Tate killers had disposed of their bloody clothes, which a television news team was able to later unearth. Surprisingly, weeks of searching by police had not.

Additionally, the *Los Angeles Times* story described the gun used in the killings. Bernard Weiss recalled how his son Steven had found just such a gun in September, and handed it in to Van Nuys police. Ballistics tests matched the gun fired at Spahn Ranch.

The prosecuting attorneys now had the .22 caliber Buntline used in the murders. The police had had it in their possession since September.

A press conference Police Chief Davis had held on December 1 was enough to make some Manson Family members come forward. The following day, Linda Kasabian had turned herself in to police in New Hampshire, where she had been living. Mary Brunner also appeared and traded immunity for her part in the Hinman murder in return for her cooperation. And Barbara Hoyt, even though she was not being sought and had not participated in any of the murders, told investigators what she knew about the murder of Donald Shea, and offered whatever help she could.

Kasabian was ready to testify and otherwise offer whatever help she could without any promises of amnesty from the prosecution. She had felt tremendous guilt about not having done more to stop the killings, despite not being present for any of them. She had even parried the Family's attempt to murder the actor she had slept with and intentionally misplaced Rosemary LaBianca's wallet. Nonetheless, she had been incredibly guilty about her Manson Family association, and wanted to tell all. She had returned to Los Angeles voluntarily, and her lawyer, Gary Fleischman, had to rush to secure an immunity deal.

It would turn out to be the best deal the prosecution made during any aspect of the case.

Within a week, the media machine—which, then, was TV, newspapers, magazines, radio, and "instant" books—was blitzing an insatiable public. Any connection to Manson or the Family sold newspapers and periodicals or created viewership. Overnight, Manson—with his thousand-yard stare—had become the most recognizable face in America.

Conversely, within the entertainment industry, connections to the alleged perpetrators were toxic. Both Brian Wilson and Terry Melcher downplayed their interactions with Manson as much as they could, a tactic that did not last very long as details about the Family emerged.

The stories appealed to Americans' taste for the lurid. But the portrayal, not necessarily always accurate, of a sex- and drug-fueled group of outlaws who led lives of damn-the-consequences derring-do and constant orgies, religious devotion, and against-the-system daring also spurred interest among an ever-widening pool of disaffiliated young people.

* * *

Manson, Krenwinkel, Van Houten and Atkins would be on trial together and Charles was adamant he would lead them, defend them all and make it the trial of the century.

The courts felt otherwise, and despite Manson's numerous petitions Judge William Keene repeatedly denied his requests to formally serve as his own counsel.

Just as Manson believed his music would cause new converts to flock to him and bring about a race war, he truly believed presenting an unconventional defense was the best way to save himself and by presenting a joint defense alongside his co-defendants, Manson felt he would have greater control.

Worn down by Manson's repeated motions, on December 24, 1969 Judge Keene reluctantly let him become his own counsel. This did not last long, due to his incompetence with legal process and the amount of court time he immediately set about wasting.

Manson went through a number of lawyers ahead of the 1970 trial, including Ronald Hughes who disappeared and died in mysterious—and unsolved—circumstances before the trial started.

Two weeks before the trail was to begin, Irving Kanarek was named as Manson's lawyer. Kanarek was known for his obstructionist tactics and frequent interjections, which would lead to many interruptions to legal procedure and to Manson and his counsel coming to blows during the trial.

The girls' legal team consisted of Albert D. Silverman for Patricia Krenwinkel, Daye Shinn for Susan Atkins and Maxwell S. Keith for Leslie Van Houten.

Early summer 1970 saw the prosecution present its case, with Manson poised to disrupt the proceedings as much as possible. Media coverage had fueled his megalomania.

What swelled Manson's chest was the way profiles in the *New York Times* and *Rolling Stone* brought serious critical and socio-political attention to both him and the Family—and they represented wildly diverse sectors of American life. *Rolling Stone*, which was at the height of its power as a counterculture bible, and *Life* magazine, the photo-driven journal of Norman Rockwell's middle America ideal, both put him on their covers. The *New York Times* did an extensive profile, providing intellectual heft and legitimacy.

The underground press went even further. They embraced him as either a misunderstood hero or an out-and-out antihero. *Hosanna!* The short-lived occult-focused newsletter *Tuesday's Child* put him on the cover multiple times, including one time when it featured an image of him on a cross, and another when it proclaimed him "Man of the Year." And in May, high-end literary pulp magazine *Argosy* ran a picture of him on its cover under a cut line that asked, "Could This Man Control YOU?"

Manson fed into the frenzy and adoration—self-adoration included—by giving interviews whenever he could, behavior he would continue throughout his incarceration.

Manson may have been enjoying the attention, but he still had dreams of getting his message out through his music. No guitars were available to Manson during this period, so anything he wanted to release would have to already be in the can. With Dennis Wilson claiming to have destroyed the recording session tapes he had sponsored, the Gold Star Studios sessions were all that was available. Manson began calling Phil Kaufman continually.

Kaufman had believed in Manson's music when the two were in prison. Now Kaufman had a chance to make some money. What record company would be able to resist capitalizing on it?

Apparently, all of them. Manson's stigma within the entertainment industry trumped even the pursuit of the almighty dollar. Kaufman got no takers, and ended up raising $3,000 for a 2,000-copy pressing of *LIE: The Love and Terror Cult*. Personnel included Manson on lead vocals, rhythm guitar, and tympani; Bobby Beausoleil on electric guitar; Mary Brunner on flute; Clem Grogan on electric bass; and a variety of Manson girls in various backup vocal roles. In March 1970, Charlie Manson finally released an album.

Kaufman started taking the recording around, first to record shops and then to offbeat stores that catered to hippie sensibilities. The same stigma persisted. While there might have been money to be made, the backlash from the viciousness of the Family's crimes would make any retailer stocking the album a pariah, even among shops that were selling "Free Manson" buttons. Kaufman managed to unload 300 copies before giving up and stashing the rest in his garage.

Predictably, Manson became convinced Kaufman was trying to cheat him. Either the album had sold wildly well and Kaufman was keeping the money, or he had not really tried. On Manson's orders—because, as ever, nothing was done without his orders—Family members stalked Kaufman, demanding either the unsold copies of the album or money or both. It is conceivable that, behind bars, Manson held more sway than when he was on the outside. Then, he was flesh. Now, he was legend.

Through a series of coordinated visits from free Family members, Manson had a pretty good sense of how the other defense strategies were shaping up—and he influenced them all to get the Family in line and on trial together. It took only one meeting with Susan Atkins to talk her around.

Manson also had motions of his own. He wanted unlimited telephone privileges, a tape recorder, and other considerations—all of which were denied. And he had one other bold request: "I was going to ask [the prosecutor] if he would call the whole thing off," Manson told Judge George M. Dell, who was hearing the pretrial motions. "It would save a lot of trouble."

Judge Dell was not above tongue-in-cheek humor himself. "Disappoint all these people?" he replied. "Never, Mr. Manson."

CHAPTER EIGHT

"I have done my best to get along in your world and now you want to kill me, and I look at you and I look how incompetent you all are, and then I say to myself, 'You want to kill me, ha, I'm already dead, have been all my life!' How sensational do you think that you have made this case? I never made it sensational. I was hiding in the desert. You come and got me. Remember?"

—CHARLES MANSON, COURT STATEMENT, NOVEMBER 19, 1970

Distractions were a key part of Manson's defense strategy. Get jury members to miss key points during the trial, and hopefully it would plant seeds of doubt. And, as has already been made clear, Manson was a master at commanding attention.

With his three co-defendants, Susan Atkins, Patricia Krenwinkel, and Leslie Van Houten, seated in court near by him, Manson essentially began an extended version of the "you do as I do" game he had played with the Family. When he indicated he had no respect for the court and turned his chair around, the girls did the same. When he was warned against putting on his wild acts in front of a jury, he mimed being crucified and the other three followed suit. He had bested Jesus, who had only two convicts beside him.

Over the course of the trial, the four defendants would repeatedly be taken out of the courtroom to an adjacent holding cell where the trial proceedings would be piped in via speakers, but where they would not be able to interrupt.

On Monday, June 15, the trial opened with jury selection.

The Manson/Atkins/Krenwinkel/Van Houten trial would become a contender for the title "Trial of the Twentieth Century," but that did not mean jurors were willing to give up the lengthy amount of time it was anticipated to take. The judge ordered the jury sequestered and put in a hotel so they could not be influenced by the media, which put many off—as did worry that the Manson Family, many of whom were still free, would seek to harm them.

Family members took to filling up the courtroom seats and staring at potential jurors until the prosecution subpoenaed every known Family member as a potential witness. Since witnesses cannot be in courtrooms when other witnesses are testifying, that effectively prevented all of them from sitting in and disrupting the proceedings or intimidating jurors.

Barred from the courtroom, Family members took to holding a vigil outside the Hall of Justice. Their presence and on-the-street theatrics would help keep the trial coverage fresh for its entire run.

It took more than a month to select twelve jurors and six alternates from a pool of 205 potential candidates, five women and seven men of all ages.

The twelve jurors were sequestered on July 15, with six alternates added a week later. The jurors would end up living together in a hotel for more than eight months during the main and penalty trials.

* * *

When Charlie Manson walked into the courtroom on July 24, 1970, all eyes were on him. Manson was an alleged murderer, possibly, if not legally, insane, and had both a natural magnetism and wild, captivating eyes. But that morning, none of this mattered.

Manson had somehow gotten hold of something sharp and gouged a deep X in his forehead. It stood out from his swept-back hair, bloody and raw.

His followers, banned from the proceedings, passed out a statement—with an ironic misspelling:

> I am not allowed to be a man in your society. I am considered inadequate and incompetent to speak or defend myself in your court. You have created a monster. I am not of you, from you nor do I condone your wars or your unjust attitudes towards things, animals and people that you won't try to understand. I have X'd myself from your world. I stand in the opposite to what you do and what you have done in the past. You have never given me the consititution you speak of. The

words you have used to trick the people are not mine. I do not accept what you call justice. The lie you live in is falling and I am not part of it. You use the word God to make money.

You! Look at what you have done and what you are doing. You make fun of God and have murdered the world in the name of Jesus Christ. I stand with my X with my love, with my God and by myself. My faith in me is stronger than all your armies, governments, gas chambers or anything you may want to do to me. I know what I have done and your courtroom is man's game. Love is my judge. I have my own constitution; it's inside me.

No man or lawyer is speaking for me, I speak for myself. I am not allowed to speak with words so I have spoken with the mark I will be wearing on my forehead. Many U.S. citizens are marked and don't know it. You won't let them come from under your foot. But God is moving. Moving and I am a witness.

I have tried to stand on the consititution but I am not afforded the rights another citizen may enjoy. I am forced to contend with communicating to the mass without words. I feel no man can represent another man because each man is different and has his own world, his own kingdom, his own reality. It is impossible to communicate one reality through another into another reality.

—Charles Manson

But the statement was secondary to the X in Manson's forehead. That X took the jury's focus from lead prosecutor Vincent Bugliosi's opening argument, a road map for what the prosecution was going to present. Bugliosi would set out how the Tate/LaBianca killings were carried out by the accused, who were willing participants and had been in their right mind at the time of the murders.

The prosecution then began its parade of witnesses. There were those who identified the victims, those who had discovered the bodies—such as the housekeeper Winifred Chapman—and those who had been in the vicinity, including groundskeeper William Garretson.

By the end of the first day, Manson and his co-defendants had moved into more theatrics. Manson loudly offered $100,000—which of course he did not have—in return for being permitted to escape. The girls propositioned jailers, offering sex in return for freedom.

Jurors saw the extent of Manson's dominance over his followers firsthand on the morning of July 27, 1970, a week after testimony had started. When the three female defendants were escorted into the courtroom, each had burned X's into their foreheads and ripped the burns apart with needles.

* * *

Linda Kasabian was the prosecution's star witness, and they brought her out early, having her take the stand on July 27. She would be confronted even before she sat down; as she was brought into the Hall of Justice, Family member Sandy Good began screaming at her "You'll kill us all! You'll kill us all!"

Her challenges continued from the moment she took the witness seat, whether by defense attorneys or her own recollections. She remained composed, calmly weathering descriptions of her drug and sex activities as part of the Family.

She did break down when describing the Tate murders, which she had witnessed from the gates outside the front of 10005 Cielo Drive. She broke down again when presented with bloody photographs of Sharon Tate's body.

Kasabian's testimony was effective and damning; she had more than earned the promised immunity. To Manson, it was the long, long Judas kiss that had delivered him to the Romans—although those holding vigil outside would hold up a "Judas Day" sign—not for her, but later, during the days Paul Watkins, whom they thought was still part of the Family, was testifying.

On August 3, the proceedings were in danger of being declared a mistrial, although not as a result of anything Kasabian did.

During a law enforcement conference appearance, then-president Nixon referred to the killings Manson stood accused of without using the word "allegedly." The *Los Angeles Times* ran with this, blowing it up into a full-caps double deck headline:

MANSON GUILTY,
NIXON DECLARES

The jury had been sequestered and would have had no way of knowing this. Their television habits were monitored, and they were not allowed to watch the news in the evening. They could not have newspapers, and no one was allowed to bring newspapers or news magazines into court.

However, there was always a way, as far as Manson was concerned.

One of the defense attorneys, who wanted to catch up on the previous day's sports scores, had taken a paper from those that had been confiscated. Was that carelessness due to exhaustion, or was it intentional? A mistrial in a matter *so* open-and-shut would actually have the odor of victory. Regardless, the always-alert Manson saw it, grabbed the front section, and flashed it at the jurors before it was snatched by a bailiff.

The jury had to be polled. Who had seen what? Slightly more than half had seen the full page, and two more saw the words MANSON GUILTY. All eighteen—the twelve main and six alternates—swore they would not be influenced by the paper.

Additionally, Manson would not be allowed to challenge any guilty rulings as a result of the incident. Defendants are not allowed to benefit from their bad behavior in court.

Nonetheless, the next day in court the three female defendants stood up and asked, with one voice, why they should still be on trial if President Nixon had found them guilty.

The girls' other actions did not help their case. When they were not responding to Manson's signals to disrupt the proceedings, they tuned out. They yawned, they giggled with each other, and they generally looked bored. Van Houten would later claim that she had been given a steady supply of LSD during the trial.

Either they were counting on Manson to save them, or they truly did not care. They had been emptied of themselves, and really were on Earth just to serve Charles Manson.

* * *

Outside the Hall of Justice, Family members kept their public vigil, kneeling and speaking to the media and passers-by. They, too, aped Manson's actions. Shortly after the four defendants appeared with X's carved into their foreheads, Manson's most devout followers appeared on the street corner with similar markings.

Others on the outside were looking to serve Manson as well. The prosecution had been scoring points, and Manson went over his list of potential Family liabilities. Barbara Hoyt had not been brought back into the fold, despite months of Manson girls calling her.

Upon getting into contact, they were finally able to make her an offer: one of good faith and fun. In return for not testifying, they would treat her to an all-expenses vacation to Hawaii, which Hoyt readily accepted. The generous benefactor who fronted the money for this excursion has never been revealed.

She was accompanied on the trip by Ruth Ann Moorehouse, whom Hoyt thought was one of her closest friends in the Family. Maybe Moorehouse was, but her loyalty to Charlie was stronger. Through Family member Dennis Rice, who had regularly been visiting Manson, Moorehouse was tasked with either persuading Hoyt not to testify or killing her.

While in Hawaii, the two girls stayed out-of-sight in their hotel room. They talked for hours, but it was not enough and Moorehouse could not talk Hoyt out of testifying. Saddened, she said she was going to return to Los Angeles and the trial, but Hoyt should stay and enjoy the rest of the vacation.

At Moorehouse's request, Hoyt went with her to the airport. While there, Moorehouse gave her friend a hamburger. As Hoyt was finishing it, Moorehouse casually wondered what it would be like to eat a hamburger with ten tabs of LSD in it—a huge dosage.

This was not, of course, mere speculation. Moorehouse got on her plane just as the acid took hold. Hoyt, blasted out of her mind, stumbled and collapsed. After being brought to an emergency room, while barely coherent, she somehow managed to say her name, her address, and something about "Mr. Bugliosi"—the lead prosecuting attorney—to the person who found her.

The incident would prove crucial in persuading Hoyt, who had once been reluctant to testify, to take the stand. But instead of what the Family had hoped for, she would be on the side of the prosecution.

Hoyt would not stop with that trial: she continued to give testimony against

Family members during their parole hearings until dying at age sixty-three of kidney failure in 2017.

While Family members Lynette Fromme, Clem Grogan, Moorehouse, Dennis Rice, and Catherine Share were all initially charged with attempted murder, it turned out that overdoses on LSD were rarely fatal, despite what the Manson Family might have believed.

The charges were reduced to a misdemeanor of conspiracy to dissuade a witness from testifying.

Within the Tate/LaBianca murder trial, the prosecution continued to bring forth its witnesses. Spahn ranch hand Juan Flynn testified about Manson's rages, as well as a threat Manson had once used toward Flynn that referred to the Tate/LaBianca killings. And more—Flynn would say Manson claimed thirty-five murders since leaving prison in 1967, although evidence of any killings beyond Hinman, the Tate/LaBianca murders and Shea was never presented in any trial.

Flynn's testimony was damaging, and Manson knew it. As the trial went on, he called for increasingly frequent interruptions from the girls. Several times, all were removed from the courtroom to the listening chamber.

Even when the defendants were not causing havoc within the courtroom, they were still generating striking images. Newspapers carried photos of the three girls walking to the courtroom, hand in hand, singing Manson's songs before settling in and ignoring the proceedings.

* * *

October 5, 1970, was the day jurors got to see Charlie Manson's capacity for rage, and quite possibly murder. After having yet another request to cross examine a witness denied, Manson challenged Judge Older.

"You are going to use this courtroom to kill me?" Manson did not so much ask as accuse the judge.

Older told the witness that he was dismissed, but Manson would not be dissuaded. He repeated a question he wanted the witness to answer, but Older spoke over him.

"If you don't stop, I will have to have you removed," Older told Manson.

"I will have you removed if you don't stop," Manson shot back. "I have a little system of my own."

Unintimidated, for the moment, Judge Older attempted to keep the proceedings moving, and told Bugliosi to call his next witness. But Manson was unstoppable.

"Do you think I'm kidding?" Manson bellowed. In a single motion he leapt over the defense table and, with a pencil clutched in his hand, lunged at the judge. The bailiff and two deputies were all over him and he hit the floor. Pinning and subduing him, the pair wrestled Manson toward the lockup.

As he was half-dragged, half-hauled away, Manson shouted back at the bench, "In the name of Christian justice, someone should cut your head off!"

While Manson was being bundled off, the other three defendants stood and began chanting. Judge Older had them removed as well.

Older was clearly shaken, but when the four defense attorneys moved for a mistrial, he overruled them. Once again, the defendants were not going to be permitted to benefit from their misbehavior.

* * *

The prosecution continued to present its case. As September turned into October and November, witnesses increasingly focused on current and former Family members.

Brooks Poston and Paul Watkins, the two Family members who had joined up with miner Paul Crockett, testified as to Manson's hold over his Family.

Tex Watson, finally extradited from Texas, then took the stand. Manson had hoped to shift blame for the Tate and LaBianca killings onto him—he was, after all, the sole male present when the seven victims were killed. But between the prosecution's ability to demonstrate Manson's mind control techniques, and the cleaned-up, youthful, and guileless image—prepped before his testimony, the college boy was back—jurors saw before them, nobody was buying that explanation.

Bugliosi wanted more, though. He felt he had established Manson's culpability, despite his not having been present for the Tate or LaBianca murders. But the actual killers had to be held accountable as well, and that meant they could receive no sympathy due to either abused or diminished mental capacity from ingesting copious amounts of LSD.

The prosecution's last two witnesses were psychiatrists who testified that, even with continued LSD use, they would still have the capacity to distinguish right from wrong.

And with that, the prosecution rested on November 16, 1970.

Paul Fitzgerald, Patricia Krenwinkel's lawyer, then spoke for the entire defense team. The defense rested without calling a single witness.

* * *

By some logic, the defense had made a brilliant move. Rather than drag the trial out any further, it had given a gift to the jurors—a look at the end of the trial. More than that, however, defense lawyers might have hoped that, even in the face of twenty-two weeks of evidence and occasionally fantastic testimony, the prosecution had not proven its case.

But there was one more twist.

As soon as Fitzgerald finished speaking, Atkins, Krenwinkel, and Van Houten began shouting that they wanted to testify. None of them had previously taken the stand, nor had Manson.

Judge Older took the matter into chambers, where he was told the three Manson girls were ready to testify that they had planned and carried out the murders, and that Manson had nothing to do with them.

Love never dies.

The move caught everyone—except the four defendants—by surprise. The three defense attorneys for the girls scrambled to limit the damage of what had just happened. Ronald Hughes summed up their general feeling when, according to prosecutor Vincent Bugliosi, he said, "I refuse to take part in any proceeding where I am forced to push a client out the window."

No matter what the court did, it would open the cases up for reversal on appeal, as denying a defendant's right to testify was not something to be taken lightly.

Atkins was sworn in, but Daye Shinn, her attorney, refused to examine her, saying he would basically be incriminating her if he asked the questions she had given him—questions which Manson doubtlessly had a hand in creating.

Fitzgerald and Hughes similarly indicated they would not let their clients destroy themselves.

Judge Older recessed the court without the matter being settled.

The next day, on November 19, 1970, Manson reversed himself. He would take the stand—not to be examined, but to give a statement.

It was decided that Manson would initially give his statement without the jury being present. Manson was sworn in, and he spoke for an hour, giving a rambling and discursive speech that offered social commentary, self-pity, observations on modern life, co-opted and corrupted philosophy, and non-sequiturs all in turn.

When Manson was finished, prosecutor Bugliosi asked him a few questions in cross examination, the final one of which was, "Mr. Manson, are you willing to testify in front of the jury and tell them the same thing that you have testified to here in open court today?"

It was a benign and neutral question; any probing question would have to be asked in front of the jury. But Manson was not interested in that. Offered the chance, he said, "I have already relieved all the pressure I had."

As Manson left the stand and walked by where his three co-defendants were seated, he leaned toward them and said, "You don't have to testify now."

At that point, it was time for closing statements. The court recessed for slightly more than a week. When it reconvened on Monday, November 30, all the attorneys would be able to address the jury.

* * *

The closing arguments would run through Christmas and wrap around the New Year. Bugliosi spoke first, taking a week to recap the People's case. The female defendants had been let back into the courtroom following the first day. Manson elected to stay in the side room, listening to the closing arguments through a speaker.

The girls had been prompted once again to cause disturbances. All three immediately began acting up during Bugliosi's presentation, and as they were escorted out Atkins grabbed some of Bugliosi's notes and tore them in half. Bugliosi snarled "You little bitch!" and grabbed for them.

The defendants were barred from the courtroom until the verdict, with no hope of returning beforehand.

The various defense attorneys gave their best shot at undermining the evidence. They questioned whether a .22 caliber bullet would be the first choice of someone intending to commit murder, whether fingerprint evidence was reliable, and whether Linda Kasabian was a credible witness. They brought up the criminal records of many of the prosecution's witnesses. They attempted to shift the blame to Tex Watson, who—after all—had been the presiding male during the Tate and LaBianca killings.

On Friday, January 15, the prosecution got the last word before a case is given to a jury. With his final words Bugliosi challenged some of the defense's assertions and what he claimed were misstatements. He ended not with facts, but with a litany of ghoulish images, portraying Manson as a "Mephistophelean guru who raped and bastardized the minds of all those who gave themselves so totally to him . . . what resulted was perhaps the most inhuman, nightmarish, horror-filled hour of savage murder and human slaughter in the recorded annals of crime. As the helpless, defenseless victims begged and screamed out into the night for their lives, their lifeblood gushed out of their bodies, forming rivers of gore . . . "

He ended with a somber remembrance of those murdered.

"Ladies and gentlemen of the jury, Sharon Tate, Abigail Folger, Voytek Frykowski, Jay Sebring, Steven Parent, Leno LaBianca, Rosemary LaBianca are not with us now in this courtroom, but from their graves they cry out for justice. Justice can only be served by coming back to this courtroom with a verdict of guilty."

* * *

Ten days later, on January 25, the jury gave Bugliosi what he had asked for. Atkins, Krenwinkel, and Manson were found guilty of seven counts of murder in the first degree and one count of conspiracy to commit murder. Van Houten was found guilty on two counts of murder in the first degree and one count of conspiracy to commit murder.

Out on the streets, the Family members who had been keeping their vigil received the news stoically. Perhaps they realized that every messiah has to die for what he believes in.

During the penalty phase of the proceedings, the prosecution represented every bit of viciousness attributable to the defendants it could. Bernard Crowe, the drug dealer Manson had shot, was brought in to show that, yes, Manson himself could not only order violence but commit it himself.

The defense brought in the defendants' parents, along with anyone else who could provide character testimony. Family members asserted their love for Manson, and his philosophies of love and brotherhood, even to the point of perjuring themselves. Each presented a scrambled story of who had done what or been where. Gary Hinman's murder had been done by the defendants because Hinman was going to attack Manson.

In one final, desperate ploy they even sought to shift coordination of the killings from Manson to Linda Kasabian.

As with the main trial, each defense attorney had the opportunity to ask his own questions. The sentencing included a stream of psychiatrists testifying to the defendants' abilities to be responsible for their actions. Even prosecutor Vincent Bugliosi took the stand to testify about some of the plea deals he had broached with various defendants and witnesses.

On March 4, Manson arrived in court with a freshly shaved head, his beard was trimmed to a point. The messiah had been replaced by someone he hoped would be more intimidating, certainly a figure who was more apt. As he told reporters, "I am the Devil, and the Devil always has a bald head." It was an interesting psychological shift, to the Prince of Hell. Maybe he felt it would be tougher to kill a demon.

While his co-defendants did not follow in these cloven footsteps—they were busy trying to assert their independence and culpability for the murders—many of the girls who were still maintaining the vigil outside the Hall of Justice did. Photographs of them, bald, their foreheads scarred with X's, kneeling and chatting, added to the Manson Family iconography.

For the prosecution's last word, Bugliosi reminded jurors that during the jury selection process each had said they would not automatically rule out voting for the death penalty.

"If the death penalty is to mean anything in the state of California other than two empty words, this is a proper case," Bugliosi concluded.

Defense attorneys claimed their clients had been misled by promises of immunity. They cited passages from the New Testament. And they spoke against the death penalty itself, including graphic descriptions of what execution in the gas chamber—the method used in California—was like.

The jury members were given their final instructions on Friday, March 26. By Monday afternoon, the 29th, they had reached a decision. Manson and his three co-defendants all showed up with shaved heads—once the jury had been sent to deliberate, there was no point in pretending Manson did not hold sway over them.

Even before the verdicts were read, Manson and the girls were yelling about the rigged nature of the trial, and threatening mass uprising. All four were removed to the adjacent room, where they heard their fates announced over a speaker.

Death. Death. Death. Death.

The jury was then dismissed with gratitude from the judge. The media coverage of the verdict exploded in a squawk of television broadcasts and a clatter of typewriters and wire services.

On April 19, 1971, Judge Older confirmed the penalty. All four were to die in the gas chamber.

CHAPTER NINE

"In the penitentiary, I have never found a bad man. Every man in the penitentiary has always showed me his good side, and circumstances put him where he was. He would not be there, he is good, human, just like the policeman that arrested him is a good human . . . We're all in our own prisons. We are each all our own wardens and we do our own time . . . I like it in there—it's peaceful."

—CHARLES MANSON, COURT STATEMENT, NOVEMBER 19, 1970

The appeals process meant Charles Manson and the other Family members were not going to be executed immediately. Additionally, Manson was slated to stand trial at least twice more, for the deaths of Gary Hinman and Donald Shea. Susan Atkins, also named in the Hinman case, had already pleaded guilty.

Manson was initially imprisoned on death row at San Quentin prison while awaiting his additional trials, while Atkins, Patricia Krenwinkel, and Leslie Van Houten were together in the California Institution for Women. The jail did not have a death row, but the three were segregated from the rest of the prison population.

Even while locked up twenty-three hours a day, Manson needed protection. A skinny five-foot-seven man, even one capable of doing a standing leap over a defense table, did not stand much of a chance in prison—especially when he was the most notorious murderer in America. So, taking the proper precautions, Manson managed to communicate and align himself with Kenneth Como, a leader within the Aryan Brotherhood white supremacist movement. He and Manson had instant commonality, if not camaraderie. Manson sought protection from assault, and Como wanted some of the resources the Family could offer, both inside and outside the prison. And in Como, Manson found a receptive sounding board for his disdain for black people. Como had a long criminal record which included assault, car theft, and robbery. He would soon add another crime to his rap sheet: prison escape.

Manson arranged for Como to testify during his upcoming trial. As part of that process, Como was transferred from San Quentin in June 1971. Como had neither a connection to, nor even familiarity with Manson's case. But that was not the point. Shortly after being transferred, he escaped and was given sanctuary by the Family for a few months.

Como's freedom, however, came at a cost. The Family wanted him to help with a daring, if typically harebrained, scheme. They were going to hijack a passenger plane and threaten to kill one passenger an hour until the imprisoned Manson Family members were freed. All they needed was guns, cash for plane tickets, and a realistic plan. They had none of these.

The Family also did not have much in the way of leadership. As of August 1971, Manson, Atkins, Clem Grogan, Van Houten, and Krenwinkel had been in prison for more than twenty-two months. Bobby Beausoleil had been locked up for more than two years. Tex Watson had last seen freedom twenty months earlier. Bruce Davis, who had gone into hiding, had finally surrendered to authorities in December 1970.

Some of Manson's followers, especially those who had come late to the party, began drifting from the Family, finding other communes, rejoining society, or even going back to their biological families. Others would keep the faith, usually to their detriment. The Family's notoriety closed a lot of doors to its members, and they increasingly relied on criminal activity to survive.

Lynette Fromme, the Family's nominal leader in Manson's absence, and Sandra Good were among those still maintaining their curbside vigil. They knelt, still with shaved hair and X-marks on their foreheads outside the courthouse where the trial stemming from the Tate/LaBianca killings had ended, and the Hinman/Shea trials were to begin.

By all rights, the Manson Family should have been falling apart, but it was not. Charlie had become a folk hero; a twisted idealist for the last gasp of hippie culture. It was not the flower children who were attracted to Manson this time. The newest Manson Family members were outlaws, revolutionaries, and mentally ill idealists. Some, doubtless, were starfuckers—people who just wanted to bask in the halo of association with Charlie Manson.

On the evening of Saturday, August 21, 1971, a mix of six pre- and post-notoriety Family members, led by Como, brashly attempted to steal a militia's worth of guns from Western Surplus, a camping and military gear store in Hawthorne, California. Roughly a week earlier, they had successfully robbed a beer distributorship of $2,600, so they were at least temporarily cash rich.

Unfortunately, they were no more adept at successfully pulling off a crime wave than their incarcerated spiritual leader. Five of them entered the store and ordered two customers and three employees to lie on the floor.

The five started smashing cases and grabbing firearms. In their exuberance over getting the guns, however, they failed to notice one employee tripping a silent alarm.

Police immediately knew it was serious, as the employees at Western Surplus rarely triggered false alarms. As so, more than thirty police officers sped to the store, surrounding it and blocking a white Ford van in an alley. Catherine Share had been waiting in the driver's seat as the guns were carried out in armfuls.

The Family members had loaded one hundred guns into the van, and had another forty or so bundled ready to be taken out. But as the area filled with police, one of the crooks panicked.

Lieutenant James Kobus was fired on first. He had only just pulled up when a shotgun blast destroyed the passenger side windshield. A passenger would have taken the full blast square in the chest, but thankfully Kobus had been alone in the car and nobody was injured. However, the firefight was on.

The exchange would last twenty minutes, with the robbers firing wildly while the police, mindful of civilians in the store, were being careful. Though investigators later counted thirty-three bullet holes in one police car alone, none of the officers on scene were hurt.

The same could not be said of the Family members. During a brief pause in the shooting, officers fired a single round of buckshot into the white van. When the van door was pushed open, Share tumbled out. She had been hit three times by the shot. The only thing she said as she was cuffed was "I'm sorry."

Police continued to exchange fire with the other robbers. Brunner had a hand injury and a bullet destroyed Bailey's kneecap, while Como and Rice were unharmed.

Lovett, however, ran but was quickly tracked down by police helicopter.

Five of the six received sentences of between ten and twenty years to life, although Rice, who pleaded guilty, pulled a sentence of six months to twenty years. Como would escape prison again on October 20, this time thanks to a smuggled bit of Carborundum Strip he used to saw through the bars of his cell. He had created a rope from strips of his mattress and rappelled from his thirteenth-floor cell down the side of his jail, kicking in an eighth-floor window. He then calmly walked out of the building and into a waiting vehicle being driven by Sandra Good.

This time, his liberty would last all of seven hours before he was recaptured.

Since the plan to spring Manson from prison had failed, the next round of trials went off as planned. Thankfully, they were nowhere near as colorful as the Tate/LaBianca trials. For his role in the Hinman/Shea deaths, Watson was sentenced to death, while Davis, Grogan, and Manson received life imprisonment. Manson was already scheduled to die.

And then, Charlie Manson received a miracle.

In February 1972, the California Supreme Court struck down the death penalty as being a cruel and unusual punishment. Anyone who had been sentenced to death before 1972 automatically had his or her sentence commuted. As California did not have a "life without parole" sentence at the time, everyone whose sentence had been changed would theoretically be eligible for parole. In addition to the Manson Family members, Sirhan Sirhan, who in 1968 had been found guilty of assassinating Presidential candidate Robert F. Kennedy, also benefited from the ruling.

In November 1972, California voters reinstated the death penalty, but it was not made retroactive. Those whose sentences had been commuted would not be put back on death row.

Manson, Atkins, Krenwinkel, Van Houten, and Watson had cheated the gas chamber.

Once the female members of the Manson Family became lifers, a number of privileges opened up to them, including recreational therapy, educational classes, psychiatric treatment, and the possibility of parole.

Manson proved more problematic. Anywhere he would be housed would have had its resources taxed. Not only did he receive more mail every day than the next-most-popular prisoner would receive in a month, he was targeted by others in the general population.

He could not even count on the alliance between the Family and the Aryan Brotherhood for security. During the planning of the Hawthorne caper, Brotherhood member Como and Family member Catherine Share fell in love. Manson, who believed his female Family members should love no one individual save for him, was not pleased, and attempted to break up the relationship.

Manson was next transferred to Folsom State Prison, where he ran into Como, who was not happy with him. Como slipped him a glass of Tang soda laced with rat poison, which he drank, although it had hardly any effect.

After that attempt on his life had failed, Como and several members of the Folsom branch of the Aryan Brotherhood made it very physically clear how unhappy they were. Once Manson recovered from their assault, he was transferred back to San Quentin.

Perversely, Manson may have not been racist enough for the Aryan Brotherhood. As Fromme would state in a letter, "Aryan Brotherhood moves much more on pure hate, as they want [Manson] to kill black because black is black. He will not do this, and they are against him."

The white supremacist rejection of Manson would eventually cause trouble for one of its own. During the early 1980s, James Mason, publisher of the neo-Nazi newsletter *Siege*, advocated that white supremacists embrace Manson as one of their own. For whatever reasons—perhaps because it amused him, perhaps because Manson's own feelings on race changed with the weather—Manson played along, even going so far as to design the logo for Mason's Universal Order group. The logo, which features a swastika superimposed over a set of justice scales, must have tickled Manson, who would see his own scarred forehead in it.

Mason would lionize Manson in the pages of *Siege*, going so far as writing, "At this point it should come as no surprise to anyone that I would include in the first rank the name of Charles Manson, probably the farthest [sic] ahead of his time, for having done in fact many of the things outlined in the highly futuristic—but nonetheless straight-down-the-line—*Turner Diaries*."

The Turner Diaries is a classic text in white supremacist literature. It inspired Timothy McVeigh's actions in bombing a government building in Oklahoma City in 1995, which resulted in the deaths of 168 people.

Mason's fellow white supremacists did not take kindly to Manson, who they felt was not ideologically pure enough. While Mason benefitted from the periodic surges of interest in Manson, other racist organizations marginalized him.

The split between Manson and the Aryan Brotherhood within the prison was reflected in the Family outside. Some of Manson's followers remained true to him, while others embraced the more immediate presence of Brotherhood members who weren't incarcerated. Manson girls Priscilla Cooper and Nancy Pitman became involved with a handful of escaped convicts based in Stockton, California, who had ties to the group.

This was a configuration too volatile to last long. The group, which supported itself through armed robberies and other crimes, would eventually kill two of its own. Member James Willett, the group feared, was going to inform authorities on their crimes, and his wife Reni (a.k.a. Lauren) was murdered because they feared she would turn them in as well.

The group was eventually caught in November 1972, and Cooper and Pitman were convicted of being accessories after the fact in the murder of Reni Willett. Just as Manson Family members previously had with John Philip "Zero" Haught, the group claimed James Willett had died during a game of Russian roulette. This time, the authorities weren't biting.

Pitman served eighteen months of a five-year sentence and has since disassociated herself from her Manson Family activities. She is believed to have established a new family somewhere in the Pacific Northwest, while Cooper's whereabouts are unknown.

Lynette Fromme, who had briefly lived with the group, had been attempting to visit imprisoned Manson Family members when Reni Willett's body was found. While she was arrested along with the others, and held for nearly three months, she was eventually released without being charged.

* * *

On the occasions when Charlie Manson felt he could benefit from telling a "woe is me" tale to his listeners, he would often claim that nobody wanted him—as a child, or even as an adult trying to operate within society. It was personal. The world was against him . . . not that he ever gave society much of a chance, of course.

Manson's self-pity was at least partly vindicated during his last stretch in prison, which lasted from 1969 through his passing in 2017.

After his death sentence was commuted, Manson would bounce between Folsom State Prison; California Medical Facility, a prison located in Vacaville; San Quentin, where he was briefly put under psychiatric care for "conceptual disorganization" stemming from a lack of human contact while being in solitary; and, in 1989, Corcoran State Prison in Corcoran, where he spent the last twenty-eight years of his life.

Manson would later claim he preferred the solace of being separated from other prisoners on death row to being in the general prison population. In *Manson in His Own Words*, published in 1986, he described his time on death row as "the most comfortable and relaxed I have spent in the last seventeen years." On death row, he was protected from other prisoners, and the isolation of his daily routine meant that, even with his notoriety, the guards would be unable to attack him either.

Other reports tend to differ. Convicted killer Joseph Morse, who served on death row alongside Manson, said in 1973: "Charlie was pretty scared. He was afraid he was going to be murdered. He used to tell me, 'Someone's going to kill me—I know it. Someone's going to stick a knife in me or strangle me.'

"I told him not to worry. I liked Charlie, but I think he was insane.

"It was brought out at his trial that Manson hated black people. So he was very frightened when he discovered that three burly black guys, including one Black Panther, lived in his cell block on death row."

Another prisoner, Gary Phoenix, said Manson described him as a "savage" because he kept a bird in his cell.

He added: "Charlie used to tell me what a great lover he was because he had all those girls following him in his Family.

"But he once admitted that he was simply their father figure.

"He always said he was the Messiah, but he was still scared he was going to be murdered.

"He told me, 'Christ was murdered. And if they could do it to Him, they can do it to me.'"

* * *

In late December 1971, Manson was found guilty of two additional counts of first-degree murder stemming from the killings of Gary Hinman and Donald Shea. While the murders were tragic for their families and loved ones, to Manson they were essentially a footnote. Once the California Supreme Court had invalidated his death sentence, any further charges did little more than reaffirm his heinousness to others.

In theory, Manson was eligible for parole after seven years. In reality, his parole hearings were a formality.

He constantly racked up disciplinary charges, amassing more than one hundred between his arrest in 1969 and his death in 2017. Between 1981 and 1992 alone, he received sixty violation notices, with offenses including possession of various drugs, fighting with other prisoners, throwing coffee at a guard, setting his bed on fire, and attempting to cause a flood.

Manson investigated escape attempts on a few occasions, but they were even less successful than his teenage plots to escape reform school. In 1982, he discussed escaping in a hot air balloon with other inmates. The extent of his planning was his having stashed 100 feet of nylon rope in the prison chapel next to a catalog that featured hot air balloons. When his cell was tossed, guards found a prison-made blade.

Three years later, he would be busted when guards found a hacksaw blade in his shoe shortly before a transfer to San Quentin. This time, the goal was not escape as much as isolation. Manson thought the discovery of the blade would result in his being given solitary confinement, which would remove him from harm at the hands of other prisoners.

Manson accepted each stint in solitary, and the resulting loss of his personal possessions that accompanied them, as part of his prison life.

Similarly, his parole hearings became increasingly bizarre: he was no longer interested in putting on a "good inmate" face, preferring to continue espousing his pseudo-philosophy. He would not wash or groom himself, or otherwise attempt to make a positive impression on the review board. His hair and beard became increasingly long and scraggly. For Manson, it was his acknowledgement of the empty ritual of the hearings. He had no illusions about ever being released.

During one hearing, he described himself as "a caged, vicious animal." Eventually he stopped going to the hearings altogether, leaving others to describe his various eccentricities, such as creating Voodoo-style dolls made out of rope into which he would stick pins.

Despite being resigned to a life on the inside, Manson did his part to keep his adherents under his thrall. In 1973, he told his remaining followers, led by Fromme and Good, that he had established the "Order of the Rainbow." In an odd bow to Catholicism, a religion to which Manson did not have any strong ties, he told Fromme and Good that they were nuns in the order, and like nuns would have to refrain from smoking—a vice common to the Family during their traveling, Spahn, and Barker ranch days—as well as from eating meat and watching violent movies.

And now that Charlie was locked up, they were forbidden from sex. If Manson could not freely indulge in pleasures of the flesh, why should anybody else? As it happened, over the years, Manson's flesh would be subject to a lot of pain and very little, if any, pleasure. It was a variation of the Old West, where lesser gunslingers sought to make a name for themselves by picking off the top man. Shoves, punches, and gang-ups were not uncommon. And, sometimes, he would assault other inmates. As such, Manson spent a fair amount of his time in solitary.

In 1976, Manson gave his first interview in six years to the *National Enquirer*, which noted he was "[m]anacled and heavily guarded" as well as "losing both his hair and his teeth in prison."

He growled to the reporters: "I'm treated like a mentally retarded child here."

Asked about how he'd tackle being set free, he replied: "If I ever did get out of jail, I'd have to run around like Frankenstein. In the movies when Frankenstein used to run, people would be chopping him up with hoes and rakes and other things.

"You see, the average person in the street believes everything that has been written and put on TV about me. They go look at those movies and they read 'Helter Skelter' and they think: 'Wow, what a monstrous monster!' I'm a monster maybe, but not a monstrous monster!"

Manson had been transferred several times at that point. Fromme and Good had given up traveling to be near him. Their contact with him had been limited after authorities feared they might be exchanging coded messages about a possible prison break.

At the California Medical Facility, Manson was put into the general population. He faced the usual threats because of his infamy, and was hustled into solitary whenever he was the aggressor.

At one point while at Vacaville, Manson found himself in a cell next to William Carter Spann, nephew of President Jimmy Carter. Obviously amusing himself, Manson found a specific way to spook him: threatening his beloved grandmother, Lillian Carter, the President's mother.

"Charlie and I got into an argument about something silly. We were both in our own cells and he made a thinly veiled threat toward my grandmother. He said he would get one of his followers to go to Plains [Georgia, where she lived] and 'talk to an old woman there.'"

Spann also described how he played a particularly dangerous game with Manson.

"I play the same kind of mind games he plays," he described, adding how he had smuggled a length of rope into his cell, which he tied into a noose and handed through the bars to Manson.

"I turned my back on him," Spann said. "All he had to do was snatch the rope, lift me completely off the ground and hang me.

"He just stood there, looked at the rope and handed it back.

"Then I asked him to put the noose around his own neck and hand me the free end. He wouldn't do it."

Manson's cajoling and mind games got him into bigger trouble on September 25, 1984. His normally fine-honed sense of his surroundings had relaxed while absorbed in his work in the arts room, when suddenly someone poured a large amount of liquid over his head. Manson jumped up and whirled around to face whoever had done it. It turned out to be paint thinner and, despite burning his eyes, he could still make out the assailant: Jan Holmstrom, who was in prison for murdering his father and had converted to become a Hare Krishna. The previous day, according to Manson, he and Holmstrom had gotten into an argument over religion. Others would say Manson had attempted to bully Holmstrom.

Holmstrom next threw a match at Manson, and the fumes ignited. Everywhere the liquid had landed ignited—on Manson's hair, his face, and his clothing. He quickly fell to the floor, struggling to put out the flames. Manson's head and left arm were so badly burned that he spent several days on the critical list in the prison hospital. As prison doctors noted, Manson's beard prevented his injuries from being even more severe. Regardless, 18 percent of his body—mostly his face, scalp, hands, and arms—were badly scorched.

Perhaps because Manson had a reputation for being a pain in the ass, prison authorities were slow to punish Holmstrom, and an attempted murder charge was soon reduced to assault. At a hearing four months later, that, too, was dropped. Officials had determined that, because of Manson's attacks on other prisoners, Holmstrom would be able to successfully claim he had acted in self-defense.

Ten months after Manson was set on fire, after he had recovered fully from the attack, he was transferred to San Quentin.

Manson finally stopped being shuffled around in 1989, when he was transferred to the Protective Housing Unit at Corcoran State Prison. The unit houses prisoners who would be in danger in general prison populations, such as those of special notoriety, those whose case details would make them a target (such as child molesters), or those who have received an unusual amount of media attention.

Sirhan Sirhan, who killed presidential candidate Robert F. Kennedy in 1968, had been housed in Corcoran before being transferred to his current location in the Richard J. Donovan Correctional Facility in San Diego. At the time, officials said his transfer was a matter of housing allotments. Michael Markhasev, who in 1997 killed comedian Bill Cosby's son Ennis, is housed there. Until his death in March 2019, Juan Corona, who in 1971 was convicted of murdering twenty-five migrant farm workers, was also incarcerated at the facility.

Inmates in the unit are not considered threats—despite Manson's proclivity for getting into fights—and are allowed to socialize. The unit boasts an exercise yard, opportunities to garden, and even access to art supplies.

"[Manson's] unit was for the guys who were extreme sex offenders, gang informants, and all the people who [appear in] true crime books," said Marynick. "[Authorities] didn't want to give them too hard a time. They didn't care how long they were on the phone or things like that. But Manson did get disciplined, though, so he must have been disruptive."

That said, Marynick alleges the prison officials weren't necessarily angels.

"In that unit they also allowed [Manson] a guitar—but [they] also played with his meds.

"Sometimes he'd call and yell at me and say the psychotic [medications] would leave him so all he could do was drool and he couldn't form a thought," Marynick added.

When it came to the huge volume of fan mail, Manson sent a fair amount out himself, though a great deal was not actually written by him. He enlisted people on his unit, whom he called his "X-men," to send messages under his name.

Memorabilia collectors complained, but he responded through the MansonDirect.com website: "They're complaining? They're lucky they got anything at all. I can't write back to every ding-dong that writes me!"

There was, admittedly, a seeming arbitrariness to who got responses. As Marynick noted, "He hated his fans, by the way. He didn't like people writing him and he used to screen people. If you were from an area of the country he didn't like he wouldn't respond.

"He told me a big piece of his mail was people writing to him saying they would have killed themselves if it wasn't for him and he's such an inspiration. He just didn't understand that—he doesn't understand how someone would kill themselves and he never considered suicide himself."

His voluminous correspondence activities weren't the only way he kept himself in front of the curious. Throughout the 1980s and early 1990s, Manson fed his insatiable need for attention by making himself available for interviews. He preferred television, as he could bring to bear his captivating physical actions and provide riveting footage. Many noteworthy journalists bit: Penny Daniels, Geraldo Rivera, Charlie Rose, Diane Sawyer, and Tom Snyder all gave him airtime. For his first interview, which was with Snyder, Manson sported a new-to-the-public adornment. The X he had carved into his forehead during his trial was now a deeply etched swastika.

During the interviews Manson was in turn lucid, rambling, charming, threatening, and kinetic, moving in quick gestures and using his famously piercing eyes to maximum effect.

He could even be patronizing, as seen in the way he spoke to Diane Sawyer in a 1994 interview.

"I never told anybody to do anything other than what they wanted to do," Manson said to Sawyer.

"And if they wanted to murder, that was okay with you?" Sawyer asked.

Manson bristled. "That was none of my business, woman," Manson shot back. "I'm a convict. I'm an outlaw. I'm a rebel. I'm not a Sunday school teacher."

But he was also occasionally funny, if not especially self-aware. As he also told Sawyer, "You know, a long time ago being crazy meant something. Nowadays everybody's crazy."

Manson may not have rattled Sawyer, who completed the interview with finesse, but he had clearly disturbed prison officials. Shortly after the show aired, California passed a rule banning reporters from using recording devices while interviewing prisoners.

Once again, Manson was denied a mass forum for his messages...and his antics.

There were few limits, however, on his ability to get in touch with people, and over the years he would both call—collect, of course—and keep up written correspondences with countless numbers of fans and the curious.

In some ways, his doing so was a mark of progress. His own literacy, while never great, had steadily improved. Additionally, prisoners who wanted to stay in favor with the celebrity lunatic, or who just wanted a different sort of diversion, would help him answer his mail.

He also was a habitual caller, when he had access to a phone. In March 2009, and again in January 2011, officials at Corcoran found smuggled mobile phones in his cell. Each time he had a few extra days tacked on to his sentence, and the violation was noted in his file. Manson could not have cared less. The two disciplinary charges were added to the more than one hundred he would earn during this last stint in prison, for offenses ranging from assault and threats toward inmates and guards, including throwing hot coffee and spitting, to possessing weapons—mostly homemade, such as a shiv made from a sharpened eyeglass temple—and drugs.

Nor would he have cared much when, later in 2011, California governor Jerry Brown made possessing a mobile phone or bringing one in for a prisoner a misdemeanor that carried up to a six-month jail term and a fine of up to $5,000. Unlike the prison interview restriction, this was seen more as an effort to crack down on gang leaders trying to run operations while behind bars.

Even without a mobile phone, Manson was a tireless caller, relentlessly calling—again, collect, from prison pay phones—a wide range of reporters and curiosity seekers. Occasionally these correspondents would navigate the prison bureaucracy and visit him.

Marynick said Manson was alternately cautious and welcoming during their first in-person conversation.

"Once we were settled and having our talk, he said, 'It's good to see you. I had no idea. You could have been Sharon Tate's son for all I know,'" Marynick recalled. "He [was] paranoid and kind of guarded. It's part of growing up in that environment, right?

"But he was still the Charlie of the '60s, especially with language. He was kind of timeless. He used a lot of words and phrases from the '60s. It was his shtick.

"In person, he never threatened me, but over the phone he'd be upset about something and he'd use the phone to vent, kind of. He would say, 'You don't know who you're fucking with. I'll drag you behind a truck until your guts spill out onto the pavement and I'll jump on your back and strangle you.' Very intense, forceful kind of stuff."

Manson may have allowed Marynick to be physically comfortable, but other visitors were kept on their toes. *Rolling Stone* writer Erik Hedegaard remembered how Manson, during one of their in-person meetings, made a point of darting forward and touching Hedegaard on the nose.

The point Manson effectively made, according to Hedegaard, was that even in his eighties—which he was at the time of the meeting—he was still in control. As he told Hedegaard, "If I can touch you, I can kill you."

Control was not the only attribute Manson retained from his Family days. Until his death, he maintained his image as a mystic, and those he was in contact with continued to be intrigued by his shamanistic leanings.

"In solitary, he said, he didn't have any real contact with anybody. He told me that when he'd come across a spider or something, that would be your whole world because now you have that to relate to, and without it you're nothing," Marynick said.

"Then you read Eastern mysticism and it talks about the same kind of thing."

But Manson the mystic continued to love the attention his notoriety gave him.

Sometime around 2006 or 2007, one of Manson's correspondents would become something more.

Forty years after he had formed the Family, Manson was still pulling similar young women into his orbit.

Afton Elaine Burton, then eighteen, had left her home in Bunker Hill, Illinois, to be with him. Although her father denied it, Burton claimed in an interview her parents would punish her by locking her in her room. Just as Manson had, she learned to become quite comfortable with being alone.

Her first exposure to Charlie was though his thoughts on the environment, which a friend shared with her. A year later she was in Corcoran, visiting him in person.

Soon enough Manson, some fifty-plus years her senior, was calling Burton his girlfriend. Like the other women in his self-generated Family, he gave her a new name: Star. Pictures of her began to circulate, with some observers noting she looked a fair amount like Susan Atkins during Atkins's young, fresh-faced days.

Officially, there was no sexual contact between the two. Under the rules of Corcoran Prison, unmarried prisoners are allowed a kiss and a hug at the beginning and end of each visit. But rumor had it Manson had an agreement with the guards under which, every once in a while, he could enjoy a little more of her if they were discreet.

How much of the relationship was real, and how much of it was Burton and Manson playing each other, is open for debate. Manson clearly enjoyed the additional headlines he generated. He also, most likely, got a deep, deep thrill out of once again controlling a young girl: Star once appeared at Corcoran with her head shaved and an X lightly scratched into her forehead.

Phil Burton, Afton's father, has publicly maintained he wasn't concerned about his daughter's relationship.

"I've never had an issue with her or what she's doing," Phil Burton said. "I didn't have any feelings toward him when he was alive, and I don't have any feelings toward him now [that] he's dead.

"[The relationship was] a personal issue for her. It doesn't have anything to do with what anybody else thinks or how society sees her or saw him. It's irrelevant. It was a personal decision that she made and she stuck with it until the end."

Perhaps as a defense mechanism, perhaps out of true belief, Phil maintains skepticism about Manson's culpability.

"There's a lot of shady stuff that went down during the court hearings . . . I'm not saying [Manson] didn't do it, I'm not saying the guy did it . . . . [but] let me pose this question: if you could get into all the case files and the evidence and re-try him for the same crimes today, do you think he would have been found guilty?

"If that one lady [Susan Atkins] had never opened her mouth, they would have never known he did it."

In 2014, Manson and Afton applied for a marriage license, which later expired, unfulfilled. Outsiders speculated Burton was angling to gain custody of his corpse, which she and another supposed Manson devotee, Craig Carlisle "Gray Wolf" Hammond, were planning on putting on display.

Manson probably was not crushed by the end of the engagement. As he told the *Rolling Stone* reporter in late 2014, "[The marriage is] a bunch of garbage . . . We're just playing that for public consumption."

Hammond, along with Burton, was one of Manson's few regular visitors during his last years in prison, but that situation ended after Hammond smuggled a mobile phone into prison for Manson—the third time Manson had been caught with a mobile phone while at Corcoran—in 2013 and was banned from seeing him.

Hammond and Burton may also have shared more than a common interest in Manson. In 2015, a news team observed as Hammond picked up Burton on a Saturday—visitation day at Corcoran—but instead of taking her to see her boyfriend they drove an hour and thirty minutes away for a romantic "date" at a gem and rock fair.

The pair stared into each other's eyes and spent hours examining rocks and crystals, but the situation turned nasty when they were caught red handed.

Spitting bile as he attacked a cameraman, Hammond said: "Who the fuck are you? What are you doing, man? Are you a secret agent or something?"

The wrestling match continued on the tarmac of the parking lot, while Afton screamed with glee in the background—a reminder that almost fifty years after their killings, even those new to the Manson Family were not to be messed with.

Despite their split, Burton maintained a friendship with Manson until his death. By this time he had been increasingly stricken with a variety of illnesses, including cancer and emphysema. As Burton was not technically part of his family—small f—she was not entitled to updates from prison about what was going on with him.

It is typical of Manson that his last attempt to gain media glory was done in conjunction with a young, attractive woman. It is also perhaps fitting that, if Burton's intent was to gain custody of his corpse for her own gain, she came close to being one of the few women who would have turned the table on him.

* * *

During the fifty years since the Tate/LaBianca killings, the entertainment industry has consistently remained fascinated with Manson and the Family. Brian Hugh Warner drew on Manson, along with movie star Marilyn Monroe, as two 1960s icons who inspired his stage name, Marilyn Manson.

Charles Manson has been featured twice in episodes of the animated series *South Park*, including one in which his forehead swastika tattoo was replaced by a smiley face. Throughout the decades he has been referenced in many songs, including David Bowie's "Candidate," N.W.A.'s "Straight Outta Compton," Ozzy Osbourne's "Bloodbath in Paradise," the Ramones' "Glad to see You Go," and System of a Down's "ATWA."

The band Guns N' Roses faced backlash for covering Manson's "Look at Your Game, Girl," on its 1993 album *The Spaghetti Incident*.

Trent Reznor, founder of rock band Nine Inch Nails, was the last resident of the house at 10050 Cielo Drive. The house was demolished in 1994 after he finished recording his album *The Downward Spiral,* but he salvaged the front door on which Susan Atkins had printed "PIGS" in Sharon Tate's blood and installed it at his New Orleans recording studio.

Manson's influence had reached beyond music. Not including the handful of films scheduled for release in 2019, there have been more than two dozen movies and television shows about Manson and the Family, and that tally doesn't include the various news interviews he did.

As might be expected, The Beatles, whose album fed into Manson's apocalyptic madness, were dismissive and derisive of the cult leader. *Rolling Stone* collected reactions from all four group members, which ranged from horrified (Ringo Starr's "It stopped everybody in their tracks, because suddenly all this violence came out in the midst of all this love and peace and psychedelia . . . Thank God they caught the bugger") to disturbed (George Harrison's "It was upsetting to be associated with something as sleazy as Charles Manson") to contemplative (John Lennon's "A lot of the things he says are true: he is a child of the state, made by us, and he took their children [in] when nobody else would. Of course, he's cracked, all right").

Paul McCartney, who wrote the song "Helter Skelter," refused to play it in concert for more than thirty years, finally adding it to his live sets in 2004.

The song was initially written as a response to a comment Pete Townshend, main songwriter for The Who, said about his group's song "I Can See for Miles" being the loudest, rawest song the band ever recorded. McCartney took the comment as a good-natured challenge, and penned his song as a partial "fuck you" to critics who had dismissed him as being unable to write anything other than whimsical pop.

However, McCartney's title and lyric were about as innocent and far removed from sex and drugs and rock 'n roll as they could be as they described a children's twisting slide ride, found on piers and English amusement parks.

"[T]here had been some funny little misinterpretations [of various Beatles songs], but they were all harmless and just a bit of a laugh," McCartney has said.

"There was this horrific interpretation of it all," McCartney continued. "But it was nothing to do with us. What can you do?"

CHAPTER TEN

"I have reflected your society in yourselves, right back at yourselves, and each one of these young girls was without a home. Each one of these young boys was without a home. I showed them the best I could what I would do as a father, as a human being, so they would be responsible to themselves and not to be weak and not to lean on me. And I have told them many times, I don't want no weak people around me."

—CHARLES MANSON, COURT STATEMENT, NOVEMBER 19, 1970

Charles Manson's death came in drawn-out silence, in stark contrast to how the rest of his life was lived.

On January 1, 2017, Manson was taken from the California State Prison in Corcoran to Mercy Hospital in Bakersfield. He was suffering from gastrointestinal bleeding and was too frail to be considered a candidate for surgery. He stayed for five days before being returned to the prison.

Tenacious and pugnacious till the end, Manson held on to life until November 19 of that year. He had been taken back to the hospital, where he succumbed to cardiac arrest that was the result of both colon cancer and respiratory failure, aged eighty-three.

Even in his death throes, Manson's legendary anger persisted even as doctors were trying to save his life.

An eyewitness at the Mercy Hospital in Bakersfield, California, explained:

"They were in the middle of a procedure when Manson woke up, enraged.

"He went berserk, ripped off his hospital armband and attacked the doctors who were trying to subdue him!

"He was clawing at his smock. Guards came flooding into the room! It was a big commotion. Hospital security around Manson was extremely tight."

Manson was also housed inside a glass room so guards could monitor his every movement.

"Security was posted at each end of the hallway. One guard sat at the nursing station and another outside his door."

Manson's death did not end the damage he did to the people around him. The families and friends of those killed with his encouragement have been keenly aware of the loss of their loved ones for half a century. And of the people whose minds he twisted, some have escaped into death while others continue to pay for their crimes.

Still others bear the brunt of trauma by association. Even though Manson had not spoken with his mother in years, Kathleen Maddox followed her son's trials from afar. The strain of her role in Manson becoming who he was took a steady, corrosive toll on her. In 1973, she died of a stroke at age fifty-five.

Manson's first son, whom he had with his first wife, Rosalie Willis in 1956, would change his name from Charles Manson Jr. to Jay White, taking his name from his stepfather. Even then, the stigma that followed him was too much to bear. In 1993, he pulled off to the side of highway I-70 and shot himself. He was thirty-seven.

Jay White's son—Manson's grandson—Jason Freeman would later say, "He just couldn't let it go . . . He couldn't live down who his father was." Freeman himself is a mixed martial artist who has publicly acknowledged his lineage since 2012. He has said his family discouraged him from asking about his grandfather, although Manson himself reached out to Freeman in 2011, and the two began to correspond through letters and phone calls.

Manson had a second son, Charles Luther Manson, with Leona Stevens in 1959. Rosalie Willis and Leona Stevens had little to do with Manson after their respective divorces, and they sought to shield their children from the infamy and public attention both the media and curiosity seekers wanted to lavish on them.

Of Manson's children, Charles Luther Manson was the most successful at maintaining anonymity. In 1976, he changed his name to Jay Charles Warner. He is believed to have died in 2007 at age forty-seven.

As previously discussed, Manson's son with Mary Brunner, Valentine, was sheltered away from the Family and raised as Michael Brunner.

After Manson died, Brunner expressed a hint of regret about having kept such distance between him and his father.

"Charlie and I tried through the years to make a connection," Brunner said after Manson died.

"I regret being very half-hearted about this. I would have liked to have some sort of relationship with my father but I looked at the act as opening Pandora's Box. I had no idea what I was going to get myself or my family involved in. I had never done any research, read any books or seen any film regarding Charlie and went through life with blinders on. In hindsight, I can see I should have done more and should have done it sooner."

While Manson's sons tried for decades to distance themselves from their father, Matthew Lentz Roberts, a musician and strip club DJ, embraced the idea. His mother had told him she met Manson at an orgy in 1967, and that Manson had impregnated her.

Roberts would later write to Manson in prison, asking if there was any possibility this was true. Manson confirmed it, and even said he remembered Roberts's mother.

Unfortunately, this wasn't true. Roberts took DNA tests and they showed conclusively there was no link between himself and Manson.

While he still believed in the link, Roberts claimed he wanted to spread the positive aspects of Manson's philosophies: "I will certainly promote his message, but it will be a nonviolent revolution of consciousness and the evolution of the human spirit."

Matthew also got involved in the huge court fight over who was Manson's rightful heir, and who could claim his body for burial. As Manson lay on ice, slowly decomposing at the coroner's office, mud between the various family claimants started to fly.

First, a memorabilia collector, Michael Channels, launched his bid based on a will he produced, which some claimed was invalid. Then Jason Freeman stepped forward. His story of being Manson's grandson had been questioned by many in his inner circle over time, and he has always refused to take a DNA test to prove his rightful position. However, he allowed that if the court ordered it, he would.

Brunner, who is undoubtedly Manson's boy, also launched a challenge, but this was legally complicated by the fact he had been adopted by the grandparents who raised him. After much court drama Freeman was given permission to collect the body, without taking a DNA test. At the time of writing in August 2019, it has still not conclusively been proven he is Manson's grandson.

Almost four months after his death, in March 2018, Charles Manson's funeral was held in Porterville, California.

The funeral was attended by around 25 people including Burton, Hammond, pen pal John Michael "JJ" Jones—who insisted on kissing the corpse—and Sandra Good, the only original Family member to attend.

Freeman was criticized for shooting a documentary at the funeral, which Manson fans later claimed was a case of his "cashing in" on the death.

In response, Freeman said, "The funeral was definitely an intense setting. The whole thing from start to finish was rough. It was one of those challenging moments in your life."

Manson had a Confederate flag atop his coffin and wore an orange shirt and neckerchief with a dark jacket. He was cremated and after the ceremony, which reportedly featured songs by Guns N' Roses and The Beach Boys, his ashes were scattered in a nearby wood. Some of the followers rubbed them into their skin. A few days later posts appeared online purporting to be selling the ashes to collectors—their validity was questionable.

The Manson estate was expected to be awarded to Jason Freeman at the time this book was going to press.

Speaking about Jason's relations with Manson's other followers, filmmaker James Buddy Day, who made the documentary *Charles Manson: The Final Words*, said: "I think there is a lot of competition between these people because Jason is related to him, and they want to be related to him, they're in constant competition over who was closest to Manson.

"I think Jason was conflicted about Manson and I think the new Manson followers struggle with that because they don't understand that Jason can see the truth about this man, that he was not this honorable person.

"So they all want to be the one to convince Jason that he is seeing things wrong."

In the documentary he made, *Charles Manson: The Funeral*, Freeman told REELZChannel: "I want to stick him in the ground to let the boogeyman sleep.

"Even though my grandfather did some horrible things, he still needed to be taken care of in death."

Freeman described how he had got to know his grandfather through phone calls and mail.

"I tried to come to the table completely open minded to see who my grandfather was—not the image of the cult leader, but who he really was on the inside.

"It took a while to get past the mask, the trust issues. It was gradual. Nothing spontaneous.

"He talked about my grandmother [Rosalie Willis] a lot. Not so much my father [Charles Manson Jr., a.k.a. Jay White], but he talked a lot about the first love of his life, which was my grandmother.

After Manson was cremated, he said: "I gave quite a lot of the ashes to Charles's friends who were there [at the funeral]. I felt they deserved it and that's what they wanted. . . . It's a big deal for them to have my grandfather in a necklace or a little urn or a pendant or something.

Freeman also realizes part of his legacy as Manson's kin reflects the lesser angels of man's nature.

"Prison, crime, sex, drugs, and rock 'n' roll was part of what was passed over to me and I lived that for the longest time," Freeman said. "I was on probation through court at age eleven, and at age thirteen the same. At fifteen my father committed suicide, nineteen I went to jail, twenty-one I was sitting in jail waiting to go to prison.

"This was a vicious cycle, and if I didn't stand up and receive Christ in my life I wouldn't be able to stand up and face what I've faced."

* * *

Others who had encountered Manson also met untimely fates. Beach Boys drummer Dennis Wilson swore he would never talk about his relationship with Manson and blamed himself for introducing Manson to Terry Melcher, which in turn may have indirectly led to the murders at 10050 Cielo Drive.

After the Tate/LaBianca murders and their fallout, Wilson's use of drugs and alcohol escalated. While addiction rarely has a single cause, guilt over what Manson had done played a part.

By 1983, Wilson's substance abuse problems led the rest of the band to consider replacing him with a different drummer during live gigs. While they may have given Wilson a chance to get straight, he would die before they had a chance. On December 28, 1983, he drowned while diving from a friend's boat in Marina del Rey, California. His blood alcohol level was more than twice the legal limit.

In addition to Manson, seven of his Family members would end up in jail for murder: Susan Atkins, Bobby Beausoleil, Bruce Davis, Clem Grogan, Patricia Krenwinkel, Leslie Van Houten, and Tex Watson.

All except Grogan were originally supposed to die in California's gas chamber. Like Manson, all had their sentences commuted when California temporarily stopped its use of the death penalty.

Only Grogan has been released permanently, although Van Houten had a few months of freedom when her sentence was overturned due to the disappearance and subsequent death of her attorney. Grogan cut a deal with police and drew a map to where Donald Shea's body was located, and was released from prison in 1985.

Atkins's roles in the killings, along with her seeming lack of remorse, would brand her as the most vicious of the Manson girls.

In prison, Atkins would claim to have undergone a conversion to Christianity. Parole officers were not impressed. She was repeatedly denied parole.

Atkins married twice while in prison. The first time, in 1981, was to a man she had corresponded with named Donald Lee Laisure, who had been married thirty-five times previously. Laisure had falsely claimed to be a millionaire: Atkins divorced him upon finding out his true fiscal status.

Atkins would marry again, in 1987, to law student James W. Whitehouse. The two remained married until Atkins's death, and for several years enjoyed conjugal visits. Whitehouse represented Atkins during two of her parole hearings.

By 2008, Atkins was in failing health. One of her legs had been amputated, and she was bedridden. She petitioned for mercy parole, but was turned down. She died of brain cancer in 2009 while incarcerated in the Central California Women's prison in Chowchilla.

At her death, Atkins had served forty years, making her—at the time—one of

California's longest-serving female prisoners, right next to her two fellow defendants, Leslie Van Houten and Patricia Krenwinkel. She had not seen her son, whom she had with Manson associate Bruce White, since her arrest.

Beausoleil has served nearly fifty years for killing Gary Hinman.

While incarcerated at the Deuel Vocational Institute, Beausoleil was stabbed in the chest and back by another prisoner. The wounds were serious, but not fatal.

During his incarceration, he married Barbara Baston. The two had four children together. Baston died in 2012. Beausoleil has maintained relationships with his children, and says they will be part of his post-prison life, if he is ever given parole.

In January 2019, a parole board recommended freedom for Beausoleil for the first time, after 18 previous decisions not to release him. Reasons given for denying him parole have included potential profits from his music and art, which parole board members felt represented profiting from his crimes.

Gary Hinman's cousin, Kay Hinman Martley, has spoken against his release, saying that he used up all his good fortune when his death sentence was reduced to life imprisonment.

On April 26, 2019, California Governor Gavin Newsom reversed the decision of the parole board. Beausoleil remains at the California Medical Facility.

Bruce Davis began serving sentences for first degree murder, conspiracy to commit murder, and robbery in April 1972. Since 1980, he has maintained a spotless prison record, and has served as a preacher in the prison ministry.

During his incarceration, Davis wrote frequently to Atkins, urging her to accept Christ and be saved. While Atkins ultimately did, she gave Davis no credit for her conversion.

Davis has had thirty-one parole hearings since being incarcerated. He was found suitable for parole during the most recent five hearings. This was despite a district attorney noting that Davis kept referring to "the Hinman thing" and "the Shea thing" when discussing their murders. His language was an echo of Atkins on the stand, when she reacted to the bloody photograph of Steven Parent as "the thing I saw."

Perhaps in part because of this, the sitting governor of California blocked each of his five recommended releases.

Davis is currently housed in the California Men's Colony in San Luis Obispo.

Patricia Krenwinkel has maintained a nearly flawless record during her fifty-year incarceration. During her time in prison, she has received a bachelor's degree in human services, participated in a variety of self-help programs in which she also served as a resource for other prisoners, and participated in sports and dance classes.

Since going to prison, she has claimed that her actions were, in part, the result of her suffering battered woman syndrome as part of Manson's abuse. The seeming avoidance of her responsibility, along with statements in which she willingly turned a blind eye to the fact that Manson was sleeping with underaged girls, did not sit well with parole boards. Krenwinkel has been denied parole fourteen times, most recently in 2017. She will remain in the California Institution for Women in Chino. She is next eligible for a parole hearing in 2022.

Leslie Van Houten's initial conviction in the LaBianca murders was overturned on appeal in 1976. It was determined that her previous lawyer, Maxwell Keith, had not had enough time to prepare a defense for her after her previous lawyer, Ronald Hughes, had vanished.

Van Houten was given a new trial, in which jurors were charged with determining whether she was mentally capable of having committed first-degree murder. If they found she was not, she would have been charged with manslaughter. Given the time she had already spent in prison, she would have been eligible for parole almost immediately.

The initial jurors were deadlocked, and the case had to be tried again. While awaiting the second trial, Van Houten was technically a suspect and not a prisoner. She managed to scrounge up bail and was, briefly, free. But in a second trial the murder conviction held up, and she was returned to the California Institution for Women.

Van Houten has been recommended for parole every year since 2016, but each time was denied by California's governor.

Like Beausoleil, Tex Watson found love, or at least a spouse, while in prison. In 1979, he married Kristin Svege. The couple had four children together before conjugal visits were eliminated for prisoners serving life sentences in 1996. While Watson and Svege divorced in 2003, they remain friends.

Watson embraced Christianity in 1975. In 1981, he was ordained as a minister and has carried his mission to prisoners and people who reach out to him because of his association with Manson. He has written several faith-based books, including *Manson's Right Hand Man Speaks Out*, in which he asserted that "if anyone deserved the death penalty for their crime, it was me."

Watson's faith has sustained him through seventeen parole hearings in which he has been denied release. He remains at the Richard J. Donovan Correctional Facility in San Diego. He is next eligible for a hearing in 2021.

Lynette Fromme and Sandra Good were no more ready to give up their alliance to Manson than he was willing to give up the control tactics that had worked for him—even while he was in prison. In addition to regulating his followers' pleasures through his Order of the Rainbow, he once again renamed them.

Fromme, nominally the outside leader of the Rainbow, became "Red," in part because of her red hair and in part because of her new, Manson-appointed missions: saving the California redwood trees from land conversion, pesticide use, harvesting for furniture and art, and other threats. She was to dress in red robes similar to a nun's habit.

Manson had similar orders for Good. Perhaps inspired by her blue eyes, he re-christened her "Blue" and announced she was responsible for saving the water supply.

In association with their work with the Order of the Rainbow, Fromme and Good launched the International People's Court of Retribution (ICPR). Ostensibly an environmental group, its members made assertions as loopy as some of Manson's own. During a 1975 radio interview, Good would claim the ICPR had 2,000 assassins who were monitoring executives and their families of organizations that harm the air, water, earth, and wildlife. But this was not a hippie-dippy love organization. As Good put it:

> Any woman who uses her body to control, or to sell products harmful to the people and the environment, will be viciously maimed. Anyone who advertises or manufactures food or drugs injurious to the people's health will be killed. Media executives and their wives who allow the flow of distorted sex and violence through the media into the minds of

> millions of people will be subject to the violence they have been selling
> to the people in the form of entertainment . . .

In case the psychotic passion behind the environmental sentiment was not completely clear, Good noted that "[t]he air, the water, the trees, and the wildlife are parts of the Manson Family."

Good was more than just talk. During the early-to-mid-1970s, she and Family member Susan Murphy sent death threats to more than 170 individuals they believed were causing ecological damage. In 1976, Good was sentenced to fifteen years in prison. She served ten before being paroled. She has since continued her allegiance to Manson and her environmental activism.

Fromme made her grand gesture toward environmental activism on September 5, 1975. Dressed in her red nun's habit, she approached then-President Ford as he was walking toward a gathering of business leaders in Sacramento.

Fromme managed to get very close to the president before whipping a .45 caliber pistol out from under her robe. She pointed the gun at Ford and pulled the trigger.

Fromme, however, had not chambered a round. Because of this, the gun did not go off. Fromme was immediately subdued, where she cried out, "It didn't go off. Can you believe it? It didn't go off."

Later, when Fromme's apartment was searched, investigators found a single bullet on the floor of her apartment.

More incompetence, or a deliberate alibi? Probably the former, but Fromme would later claim the latter.

Fromme's trial barely lasted two weeks in November 1975, largely because she refused to cooperate with her defense counsel. She was given a life sentence, but managed to escape from prison around Christmas time in 1987, after hearing Manson was ill.

She was captured within two days and given extra time.

Fromme spent nearly thirty-four years in prison. She was released in August 2009, and lives in New York state.

Did Manson have a hand in Fromme's assassination attempt? Almost certainly, but paradoxically the same rule preventing her and Good from speaking with or writing to Manson seemingly insulated him. If they had been in contact—and they almost certainly would have been—it was through intermediaries.

Manson would remain at least nominally interested in environmental issues for the rest of his life. He would later, with help from his last girlfriend Afton Burton, maintain an online and social media presence championing the mantra ATWA, which variously stood for Air, Trees, Water, Animals and All The Way Alive.

Manson had been focusing on environmental concerns since his Order of the Rainbow efforts of the mid-1970s. George Stimson, a friend of Manson girl Sandra Good ("Blue" in the Order), initially championed ATWA in 1997, as part of the accessmanson.com site.

But the movement was given a second life under Afton Burton in 2012. She is listed as its primary officer in government papers that declare it a nonprofit, and she maintains the mansondirect.com website which is the primary link to ATWA activities.

Lynette Fromme remained true to Manson for decades, although on a much less public level of activism. In contrast, several Manson Family members, including Susan Atkins, Bruce Davis, and Tex Watson traded Charlie Manson for Jesus Christ while in prison. Perhaps they were sincerely repentant, perhaps they were simply replacing one messiah with another, or perhaps they were looking for any activity that would represent remorse and redemption.

Whatever their motivation, through early 2019 it has had little impact on their prospects for release. In many of their parole hearings, Manson Family members have been cited for either minimizing their role in the killings or using language that distances themselves from their actions when discussing the murders they committed.

With the exception of Steve Grogan, the men and women who were in their teens and twenties when Charlie Manson manipulated them into committing murder half a century ago have not seen freedom since.

* * *

Charlie Manson's big break came when he gained his first follower, Mary Brunner, whom he hoodwinked with his charm, pimp mentality, and pseudo-philosophy.

This instilled confidence in him and he happened to be in the right place and time to corrupt the peace and love ideals of the '60s, and turn them to his own advantage.

As his ragged band of young and impressionable followers grew, this pattern happened again and again—each time giving him more power, control, and influence. Much like his early crime sprees where he was given the benefit of the doubt or escaped prosecution altogether, he couldn't believe his luck. Then he kept on pushing, a gambling man always ready to double rather than quit.

With the murder of Hinman by his followers and what he thought was his own murder of Bernard Crowe, Manson felt he had upped the ante even more.

Once Manson hailed two nights of murder, taking out seven rich, powerful, and beautiful people, he finally got the national attention he had craved. He had already ruined his own life, but that caper also ruined so many more—of his victims and also the teenaged and easily influenced people he encouraged to commit the crimes. Not that he cared, Charlie was a ruthless self-centered egotist who was only ever interested in what he could do to benefit himself.

Once convicted, his bitter feelings at being caught and refusal to shoulder any blame highlighted how he was a petulant, underdeveloped person.

He should have sat in jail and rotted, recognized for what he was: a petty criminal who wanted to sleep with young girls and have others do his bidding.

Manson's main delusion was that he was talented and how he felt he should be rewarded for his skills—which were simply, being himself. Manson grabbed America by the throat and although the country jailed him they also marveled at him. At his will, at his perversion and his crimes. Not so secretly, many admired that he'd done what he had. The microscope of history has ensured he has only become more notorious as the decades have progressed.

Manson's commitment to "being evil" and his steadfast stance against authority were his only qualities of note and make him, at most commendable, a true outlaw. And that's how he spent a great deal of his time—on his own, locked in solitary confinement, steadily going crazy.

Over time the gruesomeness of his crimes has been somewhat dulled, as we have ourselves become desensitized not only to the gore, but events past.

Manson now emerges as a caricature, a parody, a cartoon, a T-shirt. His notoriety continues and becomes further romanticized with the films, TV shows and re-runs filtering and sanitizing the actions of him and his cohorts.

He's become "Charlie," a friendly enough name and a bogeyman to tell your children about. An old crazy hippie guy who strummed a guitar and wrote bad folk songs. The residue of the killer with the piercing eyes and the iron will directed against his fellow men.

If reborn and placed into modern society as a free man Charlie would amount to little more than an internet troll, a pedophile grooming young teenagers over the internet.

Most worryingly, his personality echoes that of many successful people in our fractured times—ego driven, convinced he is right, self-important, greedy, excessive, unwilling to listen to anyone else and gifted at manipulation. He would probably end up running a Wall Street bank.

A modern Manson would have been instrumental in the alt-right movement—racist and bigoted, sexist and macho, taking in the gullible and spreading paranoia, conspiracy, hatred and misinterpreted philosophy. He would promise a better life just by following him and doing what he says. The type of brainwashed terrorists he would send out to do harm today would be the most destructive—school shooters, wedding bombers, environmentalist saboteurs.

Ironically, even the man most intent on destroying Manson, Los Angeles District Attorney Vincent Bugliosi, fed his infamy through his book *Helter Skelter: The True Story of the Manson Murders*, which has sold steadily for almost fifty years and been a big part of popularizing Manson and his crimes. The man who dedicated himself to taking Manson down eventually used him as his own stepping stone to notoriety. It speaks volumes about the society we have created.

It is sadly the truth of humanity that the macabre and violent will always attract us. While hopefully it also serves as a lesson to the cruelties of the world, there will always be a rush and fascination in subjects like the bloody murder of a pregnant Hollywood actress and people like Charles Manson—ensuring that evil lives beyond the grave.

APPENDIX

MANSON: THE FINAL INTERVIEW, JANUARY 2017

Interviewer: So, where everyone sees chaos, you see an order, right? It all makes sense?

Manson: The reality of the whole situation is, it's so simple that people can't understand it. Because they're taught to be complicated. They're taught that a world order is a great big paperwork thing. They gotta have that and this, got to take things and they can't give up other things. They think they've gotta go through the bullshit but they won't stand up and say, "Well, that can't happen anymore." You get caught in a circle of shit.

It don't really matter for nothing, dig? People can't quit cutting the trees down. You got all these big five-hundred-year-old trees and they cut it down and say, "Don't worry. We're planting one." Oh. Well, thanks a lot. Now we'll wait five hundred years for that one to grow up and give me some air. The trees are important. You either quit cutting trees or give up your air and stop breathing.

Put a plastic bag around your head and say, "The

World Order is not a complicated thing." It's not a racial thing. It's not one people against the other people. It's against all the people, against the pollution. There's gonna be no people left here in the world.

You redirect the war against the problems, not on each other. Each other is not the problem. The problem is the world you are creating for your-selves to live in. You've got to stop the goddamn pollution.

Interviewer: Yeah. It's an individual thing.
Manson: Yeah. The World Order is an individual hor-ror. You gotta realize, air is your first priority. Look around you and say, "What do I have to do to save my air?" Go to your medicine cabinet, look at your spray-on underarm deodorant. Look at the label and it says it kills 99% of the germs. You don't realize that you're one of the germs. So, stop using that goddamn underarm deodorant. Then you look at your shampoo. Your shampoo's got bleaches and ... I wanted to tell you this. Are you listening?

Interviewer: Yeah.
Manson: If I come up with an epitome, an epiphany and a Tiffany, and exactly, and it misses and works into a "Jar Rah." They'd say, "Ah, wow. What a great idea." But they take it, they steal it and they say, "We come up with 'Jar Rah.' Don't listen to Charlie. He don't know what the hell he's talking about." They take what I said and they

make it into a production, and they lost the whole perspective of thought because they took off the foundation. Do you see what I'm saying?

In other words, let's say you and me were there digging a foundation, and then they come and arrest us. Put us in jail. The lawyers come by and they see the foundation. They stand there and say, "Well, here's what we're doing. We're building that. We're taking it." So they do and then they store it up. Then, later, your foundation becomes all dis-torted and twisted and all messed up. Then they come back and say, "Yeah, this was Charlie's idea. This was the big fish's idea."

But they weren't wrong to start with. I come up in this world. Because what is World Order? I said, "Well, World Order's only what really is ordered." They tell me, "It's no order compared to how much money we're making." I said, "No. That's not order. That's money." And they said, "Well, we believe in God." I said, "You don't believe in God. You've got a concept of God you say you believe in." But that's not God. When you've got somebody that's real and knows what the hell they're talking about, then they lock 'em up. They say, "He's not allowed to say that. We can't have that happening. No, no."

You can't get through to explain the idea. You can't get through the collective misinterpretations of the semantics of the words that might mean the same to all the different minds that you're deal-ing with. When you're dealing with a mass brain, a mass media ... Man, you're dealing with many of the people. How can you say something to millions of people that's gonna be real? Without the conflict of interpretation—everything going in all directions?

But then, [you can also] just simply say air is your first war and you're destroying the planet earth. In order to face the destruction that's coming to your air, you've got to join with the air. Your army is air. You've got to get in that air in order to understand the air, where that air is coming from, what the air is all about.

Instead we have somebody saying, "Well, I don't like a Muslim," or "He don't like a Hindu." If you've got a thousand people going off in a million different directions, then you can't get to the problem of air. So, the World Order is air.

If you do not redeem your air from World War I, World War I has to be faced. It has to be looked at. All the mistakes and the propaganda that was pushed under the table, and the media keeps pushing under the table and keep lying and faking, because they don't want to lose the finance.

Al Gore just won the [Nobel] Peace Prize for saying what Charlie said, but when you said it, they locked him up in prison for it. They blamed him for nine counts of murder. Not for the murder. Not for ... He didn't kill anybody. But he was evil. He's evil to our economy. He's evil to our way of life. He's Viet Cong Charlie. He's Charlie Tuna. He's no good. He's not good enough. Get him out of the picture. We don't wanna hear what he's got to say. Don't mention his name around us. You seeing it?

Interviewer: Do I ever, man. Clear.

Manson: Yeah, man. They say, "Well, they blew up 9/11 to keep looking at Charlie." They blew that planet up. They blew that world up. They blew us up from Fort Sumpter. They did it because they wouldn't wanna accept what George Washington was putting down.

Interviewer: They're dropping bombs on the moon.

Manson: Yeah?

Interviewer: Shooting missiles at the moon.

Manson: Now, there are zombies coming out of the ocean. They're exploding nuclear mines over there because they wanna blow them currents up, change the currents of the planet, trying to destroy all the people.

You've got people that tried to destroy you, the ones that are programming you and telling you on the six o'clock news that Charlie Gibson and Diane Sawyer are good people telling you the truth. They're not. They're puppets for Oprah Winfrey.

You go over to Oprah Winfrey, she's got all the white girls scared to death with that dick. She wants everybody to fuck like she wants 'em because she's afraid, if you get together, that you might be against her in the Ku Klux Klan. Might come and hang her on a tree somewhere because she's propagandized.

She's propagandized with that Helter Skelter shit that the Roman Catholics have been preaching for the last 850 years. Of Italian mafiosos, who are all dead now. The dead is controlling the living.

The people in the graveyards are controlling our lives. Abraham Lincoln was not a good president. Neither was John F. Kennedy. John F. Kennedy was one of the worst presidents they ever had. Now, watch. I wasn't saying that John F. Kennedy was a bad person. John F. Kennedy was a good person, but good people can be bad in positions that take knowledge of what evil and bad is.

If you don't know what evil is and you don't know what bad is, you're gonna fall victim to it. If you don't know what playing out of the pocket is or if you don't know what walking the dog is, somebody that knows how will play it out of the pocket or walk the dog all over your bank account.

To take everything you've got in the name of smiling, praise God, we all love Jesus, in the name of the dollar bill, baby. They even call you "preacher." Reverend Dollar. Reverend Fifteen Cents. Reverend of Quarter. I'm Chaplin Nickel. For a pickle that's a dick-suckers land, you know, who likes assholes. What do we get back from that? Who's representing me right now is that guy who's got a night talk show.

Interviewer: Coast to Coast? George Noory? Letterman?

Manson: Yeah, yeah. Letterman.

Interviewer: David Letterman?

Manson: He stole me. Here's how he did it. One lawyer gave Howard Cosell my guitar. He represented the cross. Howard Cosell gave it to Muhammad Ali, who represented the wrong. That's the sun and moon.

Muhammad Ali gave it Paul Shaffer, which represents the Israelis and the Jewish League of the lyin' and dyin'. He accepted that Atlanta ...

David Letterman is from my reform school in Indiana in the '40s. They accused me of burning up schools, trying to save my rivers in Kentucky from the Tennessee Valley Authorities, when my uncles and cousins set me off because they hadn't surrendered to Abraham Lincoln, because Abraham Lincoln was being controlled by speechwriters who wrote the Gettysburg Address. Abraham Lincoln didn't say the Gettysburg Address. He read it off a piece of paper that was written by somebody in Rome. The Pope has always run the world. The Pope is infallible. That's why it was in that Italian news that Columbus discovered America, because nothing got discovered unless the Pope gave permission.

That's why he wears them funny hats, because it hooks the sky up to his mind. The Inquisition. Anybody that don't agree with what we're doing, we just eliminate them.

You got too many people. Throw the babies in the fire and let's continue. Either do that or you're not gonna survive. Stop them automobiles or you're not gonna live.

If you don't have any air and water, what do you wanna do with people? You don't need people. You need air and water. You're not fighting the people against the people. You're fighting for air and water, then you're using everything you can. Chemistry, biology, bugs, snakes, birds and trees. Anything that you can use to survive with, that's what you're working for. Survival is an intelligent life form, not the personal.

None of the ego. When I was a movie star, rock 'n' roll singer ... A person is not a plane. A person is not even in the motion. It's all computers, data, formulated, telescopes, universal mind for eternity. It's eternity that's low on this wheel.

Do you understand what I'm sayin'?

Interviewer: No, totally, man. It's so simple but yet—but no one listens.

Manson: Malaria's right behind it. Brain Syphilis and everything that biology can do. When I used to go over to chapel, I used to go up on the altar and I'd look at the altar and there was all kinds of bugs on the altar. Mosquitoes and flies, different kind of little bugs with antennas I never seen before. And then I seen the planes over there, sprayin' the bugs. But the bugs are not dying.

Interviewer: Did you go fishing when you were younger?

Manson: Fish?

Interviewer: Yeah.

Manson: Yeah.

Interviewer: Yeah, I used to, too.

Manson: I fish, yeah.

Interviewer: We go ... I used to go ice fishing here. You ever do that?

Manson: No, no.

Interviewer: You cut a hole in the ice and then you get a fire going inside of a little hut. It's pretty cool.

Manson: Yeah, it is. I don't like killing animals.

Interviewer: No, me neither. I've never been hunting, just fishing.

Manson: If I could do anything I wanted, if people would leave me the fuck alone, I could save my air. They could breathe it. Ah.

See now, if ... You could come in with a camera?

Interviewer: Yep.

Manson: And you could wear some kinda uniform?

Interviewer: Mm-hmm [affirmative].

Manson: And Coyote could come in and wear some kinda uniform. Make sure it's gray.

Interviewer: Okay.

Manson: Then we could raise the Confederate flag from the grave. We could take our cameras back in time to the Sons of Liberty in the Revolution. Against pollution that was started by our hero and our father who art in heaven, George Washington.

When George started the Revolution, he seen a lot of things. One thing he didn't see that he would be divided and conquered by an Abraham Lincoln decision.

Was overturned when the death penalty come down. When the death penalty of America came down, it changed all these Nuremberg laws. It changed all the international laws of cruel and unusual punishment.

All of those laws have been changed and put in markets to save our economy.

In the Constitution, in the Bill of Rights of the United States of the World and the king of America. A credit card that's held in honor and trust along with ... Are you ready for it?

Interviewer: Yeah, yeah.
Manson: The death penalty. And if you don't do what you're supposed to do, you will be shot.

Interviewer: Just forfeit your right to life.
Manson: Your right to life is when you stand before the court, we'll not shoot anybody that doesn't deserve to be shot. I would imagine that you could probably shoot just about everybody, I suppose.

Interviewer: Yeah.
Manson: Do you feel like that you don't deserve to be shot?

Interviewer: I'm changing. I'm working on it, you know?
Manson: Well, all right. Look at the trees that you're using in your everyday. If we look at life in the balance of Karma, there's Karma goin' and Karma comin', and which one's goin' and which one's comin'?

Interviewer: Are you taking more than giving, you know?

Manson: I see you cool with what I'm sayin'. We don't have the right to life. You can't go in the battlefield and kill women and children. You've already proved that in Korea. When I say "you," I'm talking to you as if you were me. I'm talking to United States of America.

America's not just Minnesota and everything like Miami. America's also Canada and Alaska. It's also Brazil and Uruguay. It's also everything in this continent. America's a continent, not just one country.

But everybody's got it in their movie head and they've got it in their money mind and their TV brains and radio heads that America is just the United States of America. That's bullshit. The whole damn thing is a state. Sometimes I get carried away.

Interviewer: I don't know. I don't think so. In what way?

Manson: Total conquest. Of everybody and everything. In other words, anybody that takes the car gets shot. Now, that means there's a lot of people that's got to have that car. They cannot survive without that car, so that means that's the end of them. They might as well commit suicide. If it all boils down to mass suicide, then you look at Reverend Jim Jones and you say, "That guy was right on." More Kool-Aid for everyone. The only way that we're going to survive is we gotta get rid of the people. How can we get rid of the people without them knowing it?

Interviewer: There's way too many people.
Manson: What could ...

Interviewer: Lose two billion easy. Three billion.
Manson: Why aren't they doing it anymore? And it ain't moving things fast enough. They've got Star Trek coming back with the Next Generation. You dig? God and the Devil, they wanna save all the people. Save 'em from what? They're already dead. The living are dead and the dead are living, so how can we raise the dead?

We couldn't raise the dead because the living won't allow it. Because they're all afraid of dying. Crazy, isn't it?

Interviewer: They're all terrified of it.
Manson: Mississippi's gone. Miami fell. Florida's gone. The East Coast is gone. Do you remember that movie they made there where everybody froze to death? The whole movie was, they saved New York. That was the most important part. New York, not the world. Just save New York. That's where the money was.

People don't seem to understand that. You can't eat money. If you grow your own food, then what are you feeding anyone else for? They're all destroying you. So, all that means is everybody grows their own food. If you don't grow your own food, you don't eat.

How could that work 'cause there's a lot of people

that would contaminate all the food. If they stopped sprayin' the bugs, let the bugs have it for a while. Chemical's cool. Biology's cool.

They used it all up the soil. Irrigation. That's destroying all the fish. The bottom line, just between me and you . . .

Everybody's raised up to help somebody they think is there. They wanna help their mom or their dad or somebody but, actually, there wasn't anyone there.

They found some little girls in the trash and everybody was crying, saying they all felt bad but they really didn't. They was just play-acting like they did because they was supposed to do that, because that little child didn't mean nothing but more than a hamburger. Because they just butchered up a whole bunch of cows and pigs and chickens. It's all right to kill those people. The preacher will tell you that, "Well, you can kill pigs or you can kill those." But then the book says, "Don't kill [people]."

That's why I got flesh and blood. Blood dripping off my jaw, talking about, "Thou shall not kill. Praise God." All that horseshit. Then a guy comes along and might be a little bit real about that, and they wanna condemn him and say he's all screwed up because he won't go along with what the preacher's selling.

We don't need no ... What do you call it?

Interviewer: The internet?

Manson: Man, media. We don't need no media. What we need is not to waste the energy and time that we've got left. What we've got to do is consider making videos that are going to endure and last forever. We do with video exact thing Mohammad did with the Qur'an. You understand what I'm saying there?

You do the same thing that King James did with the Bible. You create a series of videos based on one fundamental: survive. All that's need for survival in society, or a system or whatever you wanna call it, that's happening now. I call it, "The Mighty Right On." Right on? Right on. For example, artificial environment as opposed to natural environment.

Between you and I ... I don't know anything.

So what I'm trying to do is get out from underneath all this simpleminded bullshit that they keep playing with my life because they need the money.

And if I get the chance, I would take care all and every one of those parties who just continue to use my life as if it were theirs without any justification or reason to do so. They make up excuses like, "Well, it's a part of the State." What State?

"Well, it's a system." What system? In other words, they give me excuses to keep me from doing what I wanna do. Is somebody else doing something that they don't wanna do? But I've got to be crazy in the nut ward for forty years because somebody can't get a grasp of this Helter Skelter that's been sold to their minds for the fear of Negros?

They blame me and I have to carry the sin and the degradation, the fear and the confusion of that insanity with no rules and no regulations. Only a little wall of, "Oh. Well, that's a thirty-two four eight two in the book of [law]," or "You know, the Supreme Court judge said dah dahdahdah." But YOU'RE not abiding by what that says.

They bring their rank in. Bring the army in. Then stand up to attention. You stand up to attention, then do what [they] say. If you don't do it, then bring out the firing squad and I'll sign the order. I won't have any problem with it. If you can't deal with it, then give the damn thing to me and I'll do it. You dig?

I know I standed [sic] up there [in court] and lied.

When Caesar crucified Christ, it was established that you don't touch that body, man. Anybody that touches that body is going up there with it because if you touch that body, you've taken everything out of perfection. You gotta have that body to hold that life. If you lose that body, you have to go through the judge. You go through the court.

Bonehead. Dead. That's dead on arrival. I'm 1967 in 'Frisco from Alcatraz, standing on the corner with a gun in my pocket. I'm not playing. I'll do whatever it takes to survive. If someone comes up messing with me, I'm gonna do whatever I do.

Interviewer: You never finished your story about how police just kind of watch everything happen, but as long as it's not happening to their own family they could care less.

Manson: They justify what they do and hold the law

up as a shield, like they're doing something for someone else, but if they're not afraid of them, they won't do it.

It's like I was walking in the courtroom once from a lockup, and I heard this judge telling a guy, "I'm sending you to San Quentin, that's all there is. You're going to get five years." The guy says, "Please Mr. Bassett, would you let me fill out a report, and explain how sorry I am?" He says, "I don't care about that. You're going to prison. That's all there is to it."

"Please I wanna do right," he says, "I got a wife and kids and..." And he says, "I don't care about that." And then the guy says, "All right you son of a bitch. Soon as I get out, I'm coming over. I'm gonna get you and I'm gonna get you and you..." And I'm sitting with my shirt all pressed and my shoes shined trying to look good. I'm trying to do right. I'm trying to look good and do right and be a responsible member of whatever I was thinking at the time. The worst is San Quentin. All those guys were the baddest and toughest and the meanest and I always had to have my hand out for 'em and wait for them and make sure they didn't play none of those games.

If they got ten men with uniforms on and I got eleven with uniforms on, then who does the uniform belong to?

Interviewer: To the general. To you.
Manson: You know. You think of a thousand guns with no triggers and I got one with a trigger. What does that say? Something is wrong here man. This

is not even the same mentality. We're not dealing with intelligent life forms anymore. We're dealing with how much money you got. We're not dealing with conscience or honor or law and a perspective toward what's supposed to be right. We're dealing with actors and players of games and politicians who sell their daughters for votes. Look at John F. Kennedy.

Look what that guy did to the South so he could be elected as president. He was just as bad as Abraham Lincoln. Abraham Lincoln sold his soul for ambition towards divide and conquer. Our country 'tis of thee. Sweet land of liberty. Oh say can you see. I don't think there's any of that left. So if not, then I'm the king of America and this is one continent.

Now why am I saying that? I'm saying that so I can get out of jail. And when I get out of jail, what would I do? I'd probably run and hide. Knowing I couldn't hide, that someone would find me and I'd have to go to war with them. So I just might as well accept I'm in another war already. So now I'm Vietcong, Charlie and Al Qaeda and North Korea, right?

Interviewer: All the enemies in one, eh?
Manson: Yeah, well the other side, right?

Interviewer: That's right.
Manson: I'm the chain of command on the other side.

So, let's put some uniforms in my command. And when you gonna do my interview and come in my face, you're coming in my solitaire and the bodies

of my graveyards. I'll have sons of liberties. I'll
have the pin of Sudan war on my right. My hat will
be in Atlanta, Georgia, where the last of the
Confederate soldiers were executed and hung.
  Hey. Have you got a tuxedo?

Interviewer: [laughing] I don't have a tuxedo. No.
Manson: Get a tuxedo and a skateboard.

Interviewer: That'd be a good look.
Manson: Yeah. So it's under arrest, whatever it is.
I've arrested the whole world for destruction and
pollution. We're stored in all the pollution now.
We're not stored in the planet. We're stored in the
pollution.

Interviewer: Yeah.
Manson: The war is against pollution. The pollution
is coming to destroy you. You either war against
the solution or you will be destroyed. It's not a
complicated matter. It's very simple. It's called
the world order.
  Now we speak to you from the grave. I am George
Washington and the sons of liberty in my crypt,
[they] ride motorcycles, and they have guns, and
the police and the highway patrol are their cousins and brothers and sisters and souls. And all my
Marines in uniforms and men in desire will be the
fashion that lusts and runs in the midnight fire.
All those devils who cast their dreams within are
those little girls who've never sinned. We sunk all
the way to the Rhine River of gold, SS Gestapo the
deadhead souls. They're hanging 6,000 at

Nuremberg's grave. We live in magnificent grave treasures tray. I trade peace faves for those faves and all those who cannot behave with broken fingers and they waste.

Bee-bop-a-loo-bop. That's my baby. Bee-bop-a-loo-bop. Thank you. Beep, beep, beep, beep, beep, beep. That was a Russian satellite that just went by. Did you hear the communication of the people that don't lie? Have you heard those red, white, green, gold and yellow girls? And the whale said, "Oh, I've got golden curls but I'm only five. I'm only three. I'm just a little baby in a bee-bo-bo-bee. I'm a bee-bo-bee all the time to them. I bee-bo-bo-bee to them." He-he-he-he-he.

Interviewer: Oh man.

Manson: You thought I was retarded didn't you?

Interviewer: What's that?

Manson: I'm category K. Yeah. K-K-K. Three doctors who are crazy and old to me. There were reverend four in the accusatives at presidency. They tell you that the United States Government is not a church. That's bullshit. The government has always been preaching.

Interviewer: Do you want to be a reverend? Like there's a church on the Internet where you can sign up and you're totally legally a reverend.

Manson: I've already been a reverend all my life man. I was born a reverend. There's only my breath. My breath will survive. That's all there is. That's all the way of life. Nothing else exists but me, me, me, me, me, me, me, me.

Interviewer: If your breath can exist forever then you've always been here and you'll exist forever.
Manson: They thought India was the most Hare Krishna-Krishna. They say what the Krishna in 1949 over with the Rhine River is on the rolling boulevard. And Koreans are coming. The Koreans are coming with butcher knives and they're taking everything they can get a hold of. All you coward folks who run from the seed of an old apple tree. How you gonna get that by the bumble bee?

Interviewer: [laughs]
Manson: Would you like it if you were the devil?

Interviewer: Absolutely, man.
Manson: Yes, I would imagine on a level you could find. Bring a little girl and I'll fuck her in front of the camera. You can see my dick going in and out of the pussy and say, "This guy's crazy. He's a child molester. He's terrible." And then he ate her. Put her in a bun.

Interviewer: Hey man.
Manson: I don't have time to fuck with you. You want to buy a storm door or not?

Interviewer: I'll take two.
Manson: They're $79.99. I'll sell you a brand new one. Uh, you can pay $25 down and $30 a week. That's good terms.

Interviewer: At that bargain, I'll take three.

Manson: Yeah. You can have a storm door of your own man.

Interviewer: What's your background, your nationality?

Manson: My background is bastard. Navy, I don't know, lies, fear, confusion, prison, juvenile halls, boy schools, Catholic reform schools, Father Flanagan's, Boys Town, all the different throwaway places where nobody's liked or wanted. It's just one big fight going on between everybody doing everything that they can get away with. It's pretty much freedom in its full extent, like total anarchy or, what do they call it, iconoclast? Something like that? Iconoclastic?

You learn what you can and try to figure it all out before someone gets to you. Because you've already got nine scars in your left eye and five on your right and one of your ears has been tore half off, and you got a bunch of scars and broken bones, and you've been fighting ever since you can remember how to bite and scratch. And you've finally flipped everybody in the world and they don't want to submit to you. You tell them, "You do what you're told." And they say, "No." You say, "Why not? I did what I was told. I did what I was told. Isn't that the will of God?"

Those are the people who got the problems, who are always answering somebody else's confusion with a bigger confusion that says they got more money. I got your money trapped over here in my skyrocket, which is parked in Denver, Colorado on automatic pilot. I'm so drunk with power and illusions I was somebody at some time, one time in my life, but I wasn't nothing but a bug, a ladybug on a slug. I'm on the back of a bug that was dressed up like a snake sitting on Craig Ferguson's desk. That fucking creepy crawling rascal. It's the Woody Woodpecker song. Ha-ha-ha-ha-ha.

  So, you taping all this?

Interviewer: Yeah.

Manson: Out and in and in and out and roundabout. There's just no reason to scream and shout. It's just something that you don't even hardly have to think about. Does that make rhyme or reason for Shakespeare's fear of all the union oil at Texaco in 1948 with Milton Berle?

Interviewer: I think I need to listen that back a little slower. But yeah, it computes.

Manson: Kukla, Fran and Ollie? Remember them? I mean all I have is what I've been through and seen, and I'm just another motion picture screen, a TV act. We make up an act and play it for Space Odyssey because I landed the Star Trek in Death Valley with Ronnie Reagan and inner sanctum from mounds of State Prison. Mounds of State Prison is the Indian graves of the extinct. How do you say, extinct? People that are already gone?

Interviewer: Yeah.

Manson: Yeah. They beat them all to death. They killed them all. There wasn't any of them left,

man. They worked them all to death, man, down to
the last breath.

Interviewer: What they did with the Indians here
is when the white people came over to give them
blankets, but the blankets were used to cover dead
people that were dying of smallpox, so they were
covered with that. Smallpox. Wiped out 95% of them.
Manson: Yeah. Well it had to be that way. It's like
the world has to go through all the things it had
to go through before it can purify itself and be
one. There's no karma. The judgment day has come,
and everybody has to work to save the air or
there'll be nobody left. It hasn't got anything to
do with past behavior or people that are gone or
people that came. You either come back as a bug or
animal or a tree or something alive because all
the people have been dead for hundreds of years.
Can you understand that?

Interviewer: Yeah.
Manson: George Washington was not alive. George
Washington was a reject from Europe. He was a
pirate who came over here with a new idea called
revolution. It was a new thought call communism,
but it wasn't called communism right then. It was
called, "We the people." The people have never
been smart enough to rule anything. The mass of
people are just a bunch of jellyfish. So how are
you going to rule a world with a group of people
when you got 20 million different ideas? It just
can't work. It's impossible. There's only one person. There's only one body. There is only one

everything. That's the only way you're gonna stop the pollution. That's the only way you're going to put the war in perspective. You're not gonna stop the war. You put the war in motion, in the right direction for the answers to the problems. How you find a solution to the pollution when you can't even face the idea of not having a car? That you're so slaved into the economy that you can't exist without a supermarket. That you can't live without a swimming pool or a condo or whatever it is. It's got you wrapped up in whatever lives for the passion of comfort and murdering of the soul, to the funeral wagons, black coaches that carry the dead people around called Cadillacs.

I've got two baby blue Cadillacs, 1952. One in front with the blue eye looking at you, and the other one in your pocket, rock 'n' roll rocket. You probably didn't know you had a band and from a sunshine man, and a bugler can.

Interviewer: You know, I just pulled my guitar out.
Manson: Yeah. I've been trying to get mine back from the property. Somebody wants it.

Interviewer: They still won't give it to you?
Manson: I haven't got it yet, but I'm still working on it, man. Yeah.

Interviewer: Your television, your TV. Did you get that?
Manson: Yeah. I finally got that.

Interviewer: Okay.

Manson: Finally got it. I really don't watch that much. I look at the old movies sometimes. I looked at that little girl. I look at Barney, the purple dragon.

Interviewer: Oh really?

Manson: *Dragon Tales* and *Clifford The Big Red Dog.* I like the Big Red Dog. He's cool. I look at the kiddie shows. They make more sense to me than all them drama things.

And every time you see a dead person, they're probably not a dead person. They got bloody people and all the detectives got their important badges on and doing all their chasing people around. All that kind of mentally man, oof. You know, we gotta stop all of that. Baseball, football, all that competition thing. And I think I know how to do it too. Take a credit card, and don't buy and sell anything that's destructive toward our world. We don't care about gold and diamonds. We don't care about entertainment or sports. All we care about is tools and work. We're not buying and selling things for entertainment or competition. It's just a basic fundamental shovels, hose, feed, hay, horses, cows, farm stuff. You know what I'm saying. We don't plant nothing that's gonna have anything to do with our destruction. Everything comes in line with air. The first order of the world. The trees, where the air comes from, and everything that supports air, we support. And everything that protects air, we protect. And everything that gives us life, we give life.